W9-CLN-784

Word Smart for the
TOEFL

By Vanessa Coggshall

PrincetonReview.com

Random House, Inc. New York

The Independent Education Consultants Association recognizes The Princeton Review as a valuable resource for high school and college students applying to college and graduate school.

The Princeton Review, Inc.
2315 Broadway
New York, NY 10024
E-mail: editorialsupport@review.com

Copyright © 2009 by Princeton Review, Inc.

ISBN: 978-0-375-42921-7
ISSN: 1946-3065

Editor: Rebecca Lessem
Production Editor: Emma Parker
Production Coordinator: Kim Howie

TOEFL® is a registered trademark of Educational Testing Service.

John Katzman, Chairman, Founder
Michael J. Perik, President, CEO
Stephen Richards, COO, CFO
Rob Franek, VP Test Prep Books, Publisher

EDITORIAL
Seamus Mullarkey, Associate Publisher
Rebecca Lessem, Senior Editor
Laura Braswell, Senior Editor
Selena Coppock, Editor
Heather Brady, Editor

PRODUCTION SERVICES
Scott Harris, Executive Director, Production Services
Kim Howie, Senior Graphic Designer

PRODUCTION EDITORIAL
Meave Shelton, Production Editor
Emma Parker, Production Editor

RANDOM HOUSE PUBLISHING TEAM
Tom Russell, Publisher
Nicole Benhabib, Publishing Manager
Ellen L. Reed, Production Manager
Alison Stoltzfus, Associate Managing Editor
Elham Shabahat, Publishing Assistant

10 9 8 7 6 5 4 3 2 1

Acknowledgments

Thanks to the entire staff of The Princeton Review, including Rob Franek,
Seamus Mullarkey, and especially Rebecca Lessem. Thanks also to my friends and
family for their unwavering support (you'll see your names throughout this book).
Finally, thanks to my head researcher and pivot table creator, Dan Coggshall.

Contents

At The Princeton Review, we've always tried to make the learning process as enjoyable and interesting as possible.

Theoretically, if you wanted to learn vocabulary, you could read a dictionary. However, that isn't much fun, and it's certainly not going to help you do well on a specific standardized test.

So, we figured out how to make learning enjoyable and approachable. We employ this method in our classes, and we write our books with the intention that learning shouldn't be a chore.

Our first *Word Smart* book, which was published in 1988, showed that learning words can be a pleasant experience. The popularity of that book lead to many other *Word Smart* titles: *Word Smart II*, *Illustrated Word Smart*, *Word Smart for the GRE*, and so on. We also added *Grammar Smart*, *Writing Smart*, and *Math Smart* to the mix.

With this book, we've combined our *Word Smart* approach to learning with our *Illustrated Word Smart* philosophy: Creative sentences and memorable illustrations will help you to remember words that you need to know for the TOEFL.

This book contains 250 of the words most commonly seen on the TOEFL, each accompanied by its pronunciation, part of speech, definition, and a clever sentence to help you recall the word's meaning when you're taking the test. Many of the words are supplemented with an illustration to further aid your ability to remember the word's definition.

What Is the TOEFL?

The TOEFL is a test that assesses your proficiency in the type of English used in an academic environment. The test is administered on the Internet.

The exam takes about four hours to complete and integrates four essential skills—reading, listening, writing, and speaking. This means that any given question or task may require you to use one or more of these skills. For example, before attempting a writing task on the TOEFL, you may first have to read a passage and listen to a lecture on the topic.

Fortunately, because it tests each of the four skills in fairly specific ways, the TOEFL is not as daunting as it may seem. To become more comfortable with the type of writing, speaking, reading, and listening skills that are required to get a good score on the exam, pick up a copy of *Cracking the TOEFL iBT*, which offers a thorough review of the entire test.

The Structure of the Test

The TOEFL is broken down into four distinct sections, one for each of the skills previously listed. However, each section may require you to use more than one of these four skills. The structure of the test is as follows:

- One **Reading** section, consisting of three to five passages that are roughly 700 words each—Each passage will be followed by 12 to 14 multiple-choice questions about the content of the passage. Most of these questions will be worth one point each, though a few questions, located toward the end of the section, may be worth more. You will have 60 to 100 minutes to complete the entire section.
- One **Listening** section, consisting of six to nine audio selections, each of which are three to five minutes long—The selections will consist of either academic lectures or casual conversations. After each selection, there will be five to six multiple-choice questions about the content of the lecture or conversation. You will have 60 to 90 minutes to complete the entire section.
- One **Speaking** section, consisting of approximately six speaking tasks—Most speaking tasks will also require some listening and some reading. You will have to speak for 45 or 60 seconds, depending on the task, and you will have 20 minutes to complete the entire section.
- One **Writing** section, consisting of two writing assignments—As with the Speaking section, the Writing section requires listening and some reading. You will have 50 minutes to complete the entire section.

How the Test Is Scored

After finishing the TOEFL, you will receive a score of from 0 to 30 for each of the four sections. You will also receive a total score on a scale of 0 to 120. Each score corresponds to a percentile ranking. This number shows how your score compares with the scores of other test takers. For example, a total score of 100 would put you in the 89th percentile, meaning that you scored higher than 89 out of 100 test takers, whereas a score of 50 would put you in the 26th percentile. The average TOEFL score is around 68.

Notice that the 0 to 30 scores are *scaled* scores, meaning that the 0 to 30 number doesn't represent how many questions you answered correctly or how many points your essay was awarded. For example, the Reading and Listening sections each contain roughly 40 questions. You will get a point for each correct answer (some Reading section questions will be worth two points) and a penalty for each incorrect answer. At the end of the section, your *raw* score, which represents how many points you've earned, is tallied and converted to a number on the 0 to 30 scale.

The Writing and Speaking sections are scored somewhat differently. Each writing sample receives a score of between 0 and 5. These raw scores are then converted to the 0 to 30 scale. Similarly, each speaking task receives a score of from 0 to 4. The scores from all six speaking tasks are averaged and converted to the 0 to 30 scale.

How Are the Scores Used?

Colleges and universities will look at your TOEFL score when considering your application. Of course, your TOEFL score is not the only factor that affects your chance of admission. Colleges and universities also look at your academic performance, letters of recommendation, application essays, and scores on other standardized tests. Although a high TOEFL score will not guarantee admission to a particular program, a low test score could jeopardize your chances.

Some schools and programs may require students with TOEFL scores below a certain cutoff score to take supplemental English classes. Others may accept only those applicants who score above a particular cutoff score. Make sure you check with the programs to which you are applying for specific information.

The Computer-Based Format Used for Internet-Based Testing (iBT)

The TOEFL is a computer-based test that is delivered to testing centers via the Internet; therefore, the TOEFL can be offered at locations throughout the world. The test is administered by Educational Testing Service (ETS), the same testing organization that administers the GRE, SAT, and other standardized tests. According to ETS, Internet-based testing (iBT) is an easier and a fairer way to capture speech and to score responses. It also makes it possible for ETS to greatly expand access to test centers.

The iBT format will be new to the untrained eye and may be intimidating, especially if you have never taken a test on a computer. A brief tutorial is offered at the beginning of the TOEFL, in order to allow test takers time to familiarize themselves with the format. However, you should consider first taking a practice test at ETS's TOEFL practice test website, http://toeflpractice.ets.org, so you're not surprised by the Internet format on test day.

Clearly, you wouldn't approach a computer-based TOEFL reading passage in the same way that you would approach a paper-based test. For one thing, you won't be able to underline, circle, or otherwise make marks on the text. (Well, you could, but the testing center probably wouldn't be happy if you ruined its computer screens!)

Also, on the computer-based TOEFL, you'll have to take each portion of the test in its entirety. In other words, you cannot skip part of the Reading section, go on to the Listening section, and then return to the Reading section; however, you can skip questions *within* certain sections of the Reading section.

The audio portions of the test are also computer based, and the speaking portion will ask you to speak into a recording device.

Registering for the TOEFL

The easiest way to register for the TOEFL is online at **www.ets.org/toefl/index.html.** Because the test is Internet based, many testing times are available, although this isn't necessarily true overseas. Make sure to register early so that you receive a testing time and location with which you are comfortable.

You may take the TOEFL as many times as you like. Many programs will simply take your best score, but don't forget to check with admissions counselors from the schools to which you are applying for specific information.

Vocabulary and the TOEFL

Mastering vocabulary is an integral part of succeeding on the TOEFL. On the Reading section, it can aid in comprehension of the passage. It can also help you to identify the correct answer on vocabulary-in-context questions, which give you a word from a passage and ask you to select a synonym from four answer choices.

On the Listening section, mastering vocabulary will allow you to understand conversations and lectures more easily. Also, knowing the definition and spelling of words that you are writing down will help you to take notes quickly, as opposed to pondering every unknown word.

On the Speaking section, your response to the question will be more impressive if you correctly use these vocabulary words, including accurate pronunciation. You will be judged on your use of grammar and vocabulary, as well as other factors, such as delivery. Furthermore, parts of the Speaking section require you to read and understand a passage, for which vocabulary is essential.

On the Writing section, you will again have the luxury of impressing the graders with responses that are rich in vocabulary. And, as with the Speaking section, you will have to read and understand passages, which make learning vocabulary crucial.

As you can see, every section on the TOEFL is impacted by vocabulary. Therefore, mastering these words, their definitions, and the ways in which they are used and pronounced, is an essential step in TOEFL preparation.

How We Chose These Words

We chose the 250 words most commonly seen on the TOEFL. In some cases, these are not the hardest words that you will find on the TOEFL; this is intentional. Studying a hard word that was used on only one TOEFL exam and may never be used again will not help you to do better on the test. In fact, you can find endless lists online that contain incredibly difficult words that appeared on only one TOEFL exam; however, you will most likely not see any of these words when you take the test. We want you to learn words that appear often, so that when you see them, you immediately know them. Why bother learning words that won't appear on the exam? Spend your studying time and energy wisely.

Furthermore, when the test writers use an incredibly difficult word, often they will add its definition (either in parentheses or after a comma). If you have the definition in front of you, there is no need to master the word ahead of time. When ETS doesn't define difficult words, they are not often included in the questions and are, thus, unimportant for doing well on the exam. Therefore, studying those endless lists of incredibly challenging words will be a waste of your time as far as doing well on the test goes.

However, studying medium-level words that have been used on more than one TOEFL, and will very likely be used again, *will* help you do better on the test.

As you flip through this book, you may notice that some of these medium-level words look familiar; you may even believe that you know the meaning. However, before crossing off the word as "learned," you will want to be sure that you can define the word, know which part of speech it is, how to pronounce it, and how to use it in a sentence.

For instance, you've most likely seen the word "advice." But make sure that you have truly mastered it, and that you know how it differs from the word "advise." The spelling is the same, except for one letter, but the parts of speech and the meanings are different.

Truly mastering each word in this book, no matter how easy some may look, will make you more prepared for all four sections of the TOEFL on test day.

What we're saying is that if some of the words in this book sound simple, it's intentional. Not only are these the words that you will encounter on the test, they are also trickier than they may seem. Though they may *sound* simple, these words are often unknowingly used incorrectly by test takers.

We have made the definitions as fundamental as possible: There's no sense in learning a word if the definition is too hard to understand and remember. You can find more complex definitions in a dictionary, but we find that this simple and straightforward approach is best, and that it makes the words easier to remember.

Most words have second and third definitions. For the words in this book, we picked one definition—the definition that is most commonly used on the TOEFL. While you can learn additional definitions by referencing a dictionary, we have saved you time, because the main definitions that we present are the ones you will need to know for the test.

Finally, most words have multiple forms; "reduce" can be "reducing," "reduced," and "reduces." This book presents the forms that are most commonly found on the TOEFL. If "reduced" is repeatedly used on the test, we test you on this form of the word.

How to Use This Book

This book is divided into 17 chapters of related words. For example, the chapter titled "Change Your Tune" is about words that have to do with changing and being different, while the chapter titled "Express Yourself" is about words that relate to giving your opinion and winning an argument. Each chapter represents one manageable set of words that can be learned as a chunk.

If you try to memorize all of these words in one sitting, it won't work. It takes time to transfer knowledge from your short-term memory to your long-term memory, so take at least three to four days to let your mind absorb the words before moving on to a new chapter. Occasionally, come back to chapters you've already read to test your memory and review these words.

At the end of each chapter, you will find drills that quiz you on every word in the chapter. After doing the drills, you can consult the answer key to check your work.

Some chapters have drills that will help you practice your speaking and writing skills. These chapters will ask you to answer a question (either by speaking or writing) using every word in the chapter. While there are many possible answers to these questions, an answer key with sample responses has been provided for you. Another way to practice your speaking skills is to read the sample responses aloud. The more you practice using these words, the more confident you are going to feel about them on test day.

Many of the chapters contain illustrations, which will help you to remember the meaning of the vocabulary words presented. We hope you will find some of these illustrations amusing, which will further help you to remember each word's connotation.

Please note that because of the way the chapters are divided, they do not have to be read in order. You can choose the chapter that you find most appealing and start there!

Using Notations

As we discussed in the previous section, your mission is to review these words until you know them by heart.

One device that can help you identify the words you've mastered and the words you still need to learn is the use of notations. Every time you encounter a word in this book, you can make a mark to indicate your familiarity with its pronunciation, its part of speech, and its meaning; all parts are equally important. If you know a word's meaning but can't pronounce it, that will affect your score on the Speaking section. Likewise, if you know a word's part of speech but not its meaning, you run the risk of using it incorrectly and losing points on the Writing section.

So, to remind yourself of your familiarity with each of these factors, you can make marks next to each word. For instance:

✓   means "Without a doubt, I know the pronunciation, part of speech, and meaning."

?   means "I don't know this word or any of its other parts."

O   means "I know one or two things, such as the pronunciation or part of speech, but I don't know other parts."

You can consider the words with check marks as words you've mastered, and you'll only need to review those words once or twice before the test. However, you'll need to continue to drill the other two categories until they fall into the check mark category. This process will save you time because the majority of your studying will be restricted to the words that you still need to learn.

Pronunciation

We don't use standard dictionary phonetics in our *Word Smart* books, for the simple reason that many people don't understand phonetics. Instead, we use a modified phonetic approach that we believe is largely intuitive. The pronunciation key below should clear up any questions you may have about how to use our pronunciation guide:

The letter(s)	is (are) pronounced like the letter(s)	in the word(s)
a	a	bat, can
ah	o	con, on
aw	aw	paw, straw
ay	a	skate, rake
e	e	stem, hem, err
ee	ea	steam, clean
i	i	rim, chin, hint
ing	ing	sing, ring
oh	o	row, tow
oo	oo	room, boom
ow	ow	cow, brow
oy	oy	boy, toy
u, uh	u	run, bun
y (ye, eye)	i	climb, time
ch	ch	chair, chin
f	f, ph	film, phony
g	g	go, goon
j	j	join, jungle
k	c	cool, cat
s	s	solid, wisp
sh	sh	shoe, wish
z	z	zoo, razor
zh	s	measure

All other consonants are pronounced as you would expect. Capitalized letters are the part of the word that you pronounce with emphasis, or accent.

Other Ways to Boost Your Vocabulary

In addition to working with this book, there are other ways that you can enhance your vocabulary on a daily basis; learning new words and using them correctly will be beneficial to you on every section of the TOEFL (and in real life!).

Here are some other ways you can boost your vocabulary:

- Read magazines such as *Time, Discover, Entertainment Weekly, Sports Illustrated,* and news papers such as *USA Today* or *The New York Times*. This will help your comprehension as well as your vocabulary.
- Watch television and listen to the radio. These are enjoyable ways to learn the language! Almost any show or program will be helpful.
- Do a quick search on the Internet to find a number of helpful websites which are devoted to helping people learn English. You can even find online dictionaries with audio that will demonstrate how to pronounce new words.
- Make an effort to engage in conversation using words that you are still in the process of learning. You can even chat with people online to try out your new vocabulary.
- When you hear a word that you don't know, write it down immediately. Come back to it later and do three things:
  (1) Look up the word in the dictionary and write down on a flashcard its pronunciation, part of speech, and definition.
  (2) Make a sentence using that word.
  (3) Continue to review the flashcard until you know all the parts of your new word and can use it in a sentence.

What Is the Princeton Review?

The Princeton Review is *the* premier test-preparation company; we prepare tens of thousands of students each year for tests such as the TOEFL, SAT, GMAT, GRE, LSAT, and MCAT. At The Princeton Review, we spend countless hours researching tests and figuring out exactly how to crack them. We offer students proven, high-powered strategies and techniques that help them beat the tests and achieve their best scores.

In addition to our books, we offer both live classroom instruction and online courses. If you would like more information about our programs, visit us at **PrincetonReview.com.**

If you are looking for information on Princeton Review courses offered outside the United States, go to www.princetonreview.com/international-locations.aspx.

CHAPTER 1
CHANGE YOUR TUNE
Words about changing and being different

ADAPT (uh DAPT) *v* to change in order to better handle a situation

Even though I dislike camping in the woods, I decided that the best way to *adapt* to my surroundings was to sleep in a tent instead of in my car.

AFFECT (uh FEKT) *v* to cause change in something

I know that drinking coffee will *affect* my energy level, so tonight I will drink twelve cups and get all of my work done.

ALTERNATIVE (awl TUR nuh tiv) *n* an option; something that you can choose instead of something else

The heater in my house is not working, so I must use an *alternative* way to warm myself, like blankets.

DIVERSITY (di VUR si tee) *n* variety; a state of difference

The *diversity* of the senior class became clear when we all chose different career paths.

EVOLVE (ee VAHLV) *v* to develop or get better slowly

It is true that Cro-Magnon man did not have the capacity to under-stand that he would *evolve* into today's human being.

EXPERIMENT (eks PEER uh ment) *n* a scientific test or trial

The physics student described the arc of an object in flight with an *experiment* that involved a baseball.

/flʌctʃueɪt/ v,上下波动;起伏

FLUCTUATE (FLUHK choo eyt) *v* to change or move back and forth

It was difficult for me to decide whether I should purchase a laptop or a desktop computer, because my needs *fluctuate*.

IMPROVE (im PROOV) *v* to make better

The professor said that I can *improve* my resume by doing an internship at a marketing firm.

INNOVATIONS (in uh VEY shuhns) *n* advances or improvements in various areas of life

Thomas Edison was responsible for many *innovations* in addition to the light bulb.

/ˈmaɪɡreɪt/ 迁徙：迁移（计算机系统）通新

MIGRATE (MYE grayt) *v* to move from one place to another

Because they get cold up North, birds *migrate* to the South for the winter.

/from

REDUCED (ri DOOSD) *v* made less or smaller

I was very excited about the sale at the university bookstore because all of the prices had been *reduced*.

REPLACED (ri PLEYSD) *v* changed one with another

Thrilled that she got her first paycheck, Cari immediately *replaced* her old cell phone with a newer model.

非常兴奋的　　　　　工资

RESIST (ri ZIST) *v* to fight against

The criminal attempted to *resist* arrest by running at full speed and not looking back.

TRANSFORMED (trans FOHRMD) *v* changed

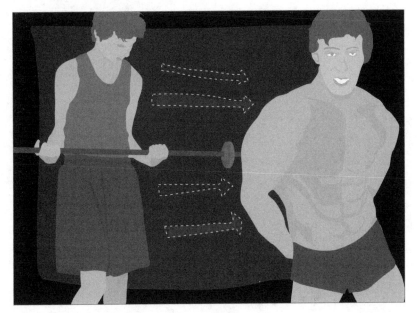

David, who was unhappy with his appearance, started going to the gym and was *transformed* into someone with very large muscles.

VARY (VER ee) *v* to change

Ivan chose to *vary* his work schedule by coming in on Wednesdays instead of Fridays.

DRILLS

Quiz #1

Match each word in the first column with its definition in the second column.

1. Migrate
2. Transformed
3. Adapt
4. Reduced
5. Experiment
6. Evolve
7. Vary
8. Alternative
9. Affect
10. Improve
11. Fluctuate
12. Resist
13. Diversity
14. Innovations
15. Replaced

a. an option; something that you can choose instead
b. made smaller
c. to fight against
d. to make better
e. to move from one place to another
f. variety; a state of difference
g. changed
h. changed one with another
i. advances or improvements in various areas of life
j. to cause change in something
k. a scientific test or trial
l. to change or move back and forth
m. to change
n. to change in order to better handle a situation
o. to develop or get better slowly

Puzzle #1

Using the definitions below, figure out which words you are looking for, and then circle them in the Word Search. The words are spelled up, down, diagonally, and backwards.

```
W  I  N  I  G  K  I  B  G  Q  T  W  U  F  P
E  U  U  F  N  Z  W  H  U  F  P  O  L  U  U
E  V  I  T  A  N  R  E  T  L  A  B  H  N  A
M  X  O  B  R  O  O  P  V  V  D  B  S  F  W
J  R  P  L  Y  A  N  V  E  O  A  N  K  W  E
S  K  H  B  V  D  N  W  A  P  R  B  Z  L  C
D  J  D  I  V  E  R  S  I  T  Y  P  A  T  I
E  T  A  U  T  C  U  L  F  R  I  U  M  M  A
R  M  I  G  R  A  T  E  J  O  E  O  G  I  S
S  I  M  B  E  L  F  M  V  A  R  Y  N  N  J
D  O  V  C  D  P  F  F  S  K  M  M  Z  S  S
N  A  C  P  U  E  X  P  E  R  I  M  E  N  T
T  G  W  A  C  R  L  N  M  C  H  J  R  D  I
E  U  J  R  E  S  I  S  T  L  T  G  N  M  M
K  M  O  S  D  P  J  W  L  X  N  M  K  R  I
```

Definitions:
1. to change in order to better handle a situation
2. to cause change in something
3. an option; something that you can choose instead
4. variety; a state of difference
5. to develop or get better slowly
6. a scientific test or trial
7. to change or move back and forth
8. to make better
9. advances or improvements in various areas of life
10. to move from one place to another
11. made smaller
12. changed one with another
13. to fight against
14. changed
15. to change

Quiz #1 Answer Key:

1. e
2. g
3. n
4. b
5. k
6. o
7. m
8. a
9. j
10. d
11. l
12. c
13. f
14. i
15. h

Puzzle #1 Answer Key:

```
W  I  N  I  G  K  I  B  G  Q  T  W  U  F  P
E  U  U  F  N  Z  W  H  U  F  P  O  L  U  U
E  V  I  T  A  N  R  E  T  L  A  B  H  N  A
M  X  O  B  R  O  O  P  V  V  D  B  S  F  W
J  R  P  L  Y  A  N  V  E  O  A  N  K  W  E
S  K  H  B  V  D  N  W  A  P  R  B  Z  L  C
D  J  D  I  V  E  R  S  I  T  Y  P  A  T  I
E  T  A  U  T  C  U  L  F  R  I  U  M  M  A
R  M  I  G  R  A  T  E  J  O  E  O  G  I  S
S  I  M  B  E  L  F  M  V  A  R  Y  N  N  J
D  O  V  C  D  P  F  F  S  K  M  M  Z  S  S
N  A  C  P  U  E  X  P  E  R  I  M  E  N  T
T  G  W  A  C  R  L  N  M  C  H  J  R  D  I
E  U  J  R  E  S  I  S  T  L  T  G  N  M  M
K  M  O  S  D  P  J  W  L  X  N  M  K  R  I
```

(Over, Down, Direction)

1. Adapt (11, 5, N)
2. Affect (6, 9, SE)
3. Alternative (11, 3, W)
4. Diversity (3, 7, E)
5. Evolve (1, 2, SE)
6. Experiment (6, 12, E)
7. Fluctuate (9, 8, W)
8. Improve (14, 9, NW)
9. Innovations (4, 1, SE)
10. Migrate (2, 9, E)
11. Reduced (5, 9, S)
12. Replaced (6, 13, N)
13. Resist (4, 14, E)
14. Transformed (4, 3, SE)
15. Vary (9, 10, E)

CHAPTER 2
EXPRESS YOURSELF

Words about giving an opinion and winning an argument

ADVANTAGE (ad VAN tij) *n* a benefit; a better position

Our team had the *advantage* in the basketball game because one of our players is seven feet tall.

APPEAL (uh PEEL) *n* a request for help

Because my grades were suffering, I made an *appeal* to my professor and asked for extra help.

ARGUE (AHR gyoo) *v* to state that you agree or disagree with something

The lawyer tried to *argue* that his client ran away because he has a phobia of police sirens.

CONFLICT (kuhn FLIKT) *v* to fight; disagree

I must point out that your arguments *conflict* with the author's thesis.

CONTRADICT (kon truh DIKT) *v* to give an opposite statement

It makes me angry when you *contradict* everything I say.

CONVINCE (kuhn VINS) *v* to make someone believe in something

Hong was able to *convince* her husband to buy a new car to match her dress.

CRITICAL (KRIT i kuhl) *adj* judgemental

The *critical* bride told her bridesmaids that their dresses were too short and told the florist that the flowers were ugly.

ENCOURAGE (en KUR ij) *v* to inspire with hope

Lisa's boss tried to *encourage* her to take on more responsibilities by telling her she would make more money.

ENSURE (en SHOOR) *v* to make sure or certain

To *ensure* that you will remember to meet me at the basketball game tonight, I am giving you the tickets in advance.

EXCEPT (ik SEPT) *prep* leaving out; instead of; everything but

Unfortunately, the limousine driver was able to fit everyone in the car *except* for me, so I had to walk home.

OPPOSE (uh POHZ) *v* to go against; disagree with

Many people *oppose* animal testing and, therefore, check the label before purchasing a bottle of shampoo .

PREVENT (pri VENT) *v* to stop from happening

The bodyguard's job was to *prevent* anyone from coming close to the President.

(

PROMOTE (pruh MOHT) *v* to help; to speak in favor of

The record label wanted to *promote* their new star, so they had him appear on every talk show.

PROVE (proov) *v* to show to be true

I entered a smiling contest to *prove* that I had the prettiest smile in town.

DRILLS

Quiz #1

Match each word in the first column with its definition in the second column.

1. Prove
2. Oppose
3. Contradict
4. Prevent
5. Convince
6. Ensure
7. Conflict
8. Critical
9. Encourage
10. Appeal
11. Except
12. Argue
13. Advantage
14. Promote

a. to make someone believe in something
b. to help; to speak in favor of
c. judgmental
d. a benefit; a better position
e. to inspire with hope
f. to fight; disagree
g. to make sure or certain
h. to give an opposite statement
i. leaving out; instead of
j. a request for help
k. to go against; disagree with
l. to stop from happening
m. to state that you agree or disagree with something
n. to show to be true

Quiz #2

Practice your speaking skills by answering the following question aloud. Use every word from this chapter in your response.

Question: Some people believe it is important to forgive and forget. Others are more likely to hold a grudge. Which approach do you think is better and why?

Use all of these words in your response:

Advantage	Appeal
Argue	Conflict
Contradict	Convince
Critical	Encourage
Ensure	Except
Oppose	Prevent
Promote	Prove

_____

_____

_____

_____

_____

_____

_____

_____

_____

_____

_____

_____

_____

_____

_____

_____

_____

_____

_____

_____

_____

_____

_____

_____

Puzzle #1

Across

2. Judgemental
7. To help; to speak in favor of
10. To show to be true
11. To inspire with hope
12. To give an opposite statement
13. To make sure or certain

Down

1. A request for help
3. To make someone believe in something
4. To fight; disagree
5. To go against; disagree with
6. Leaving out; instead of
8. To state that you agree or disagree with something
9. A benefit; a better position
10. To stop from happening

Quiz #1 Answer Key:

1. n
2. k
3. h
4. l
5. a
6. g
7. f
8. c
9. e
10. j
11. i
12. m
13. d
14. b

Quiz #2 Answer Key:

There are many possible responses to this task. Here is a sample response that you can read aloud to practice your speaking skills.

I would have to **argue** that, if someone has wronged you in the past, you should forgive and forget instead of holding a grudge. There are many reasons for my opinion. First, your kindness would **encourage** the other person to **prevent** any wrongdoings in the future. Also, it would **ensure** that this person learns from his or her mistakes and would **promote** a sense of knowing what is right and wrong.

However, someone who would **oppose** the belief that you should forgive and forget would **contradict** my opinion and try to **convince** you that people never change, **except** in rare circumstances. This **critical** approach to the question would **conflict** with my theory that there is an **advantage** to showing others what is right and wrong.

Though I can **prove** that my approach is more beneficial because i have saved many friendships by forgiving and forgetting wrongdoings. So I would like to **appeal** to those who disagree with me and request that they at least consider my point of view.

Puzzle #1 Answer Key:

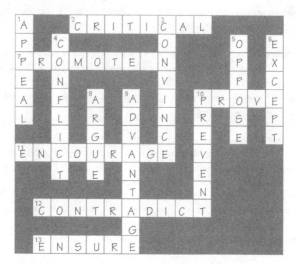

CHAPTER 3
THINK IT OVER

Words about the process of reasoning and reflecting

ANALYSIS (uh NAL uh sis) *n* a study of the basics of something

An accountant did an *analysis* of my finances and, after looking over all the data, concluded that I am poor.

AWARE (uh WAIR) *adj* having knowledge

After thinking hard about why I did not have enough time for my schoolwork, I became *aware* that I watch too much television.

BELIEF (bi LEEF) *n* an opinion; faith in something

Most teachers hold a strong *belief* that if one reads every day, one will expand his or her vocabulary.

CONCENTRATE (KON suhn treyt) *v* to think hard about

While taking the test, Giacomo found it easiest to *concentrate* if he put his fingers in his ears to block out all noise.

CONCEPT (KON sept) *n* an idea

Even though the professor explained the *concept* of string theory for an entire lecture, I was still confused.

CONSIDER (kuhn SID er) *v* to think about something

Before you fall in love with that painting, I think you should *consider* the large price tag on it.

DECISION (di SIZH uhn) *n* a final choice

Even though he would have to dress up like a giant lizard, the movie star made the *decision* to accept the role.

ESTIMATE (ES tuh meyt) *v* to guess based on knowledge

Based on my research, I *estimate* that a person can live without water for eleven days.

INFERRED (in FURD) *v* guessed based on hints

I *inferred* from his clothes that he was a basketball player.

OBJECTIVE (uhb JEK tiv) *n* a goal or purpose

The *objective* of my presentation was to show the class how to play the drums.

OPINION (uh PIN yuhn) *n* a personal view or thought

Aggie is a connoisseur of hamburgers so, when sampling them at various restaurants, she always voices her *opinion*.

REFLECTED (re FLEK tid) *v* to show or think back

To prepare herself for the upcoming race, Jodi *reflected* on her coach's words of encouragement.

SOPHISTICATED (suh FIS ti key tid) *adj* having high-class tastes; cultured

I wanted to appear more *sophisticated* at work, so I started wearing business suits and glasses.

THEORY (THEER ee) *n* an idea that something is true

Shannon has a *theory* that it always rains on days when she forgets her umbrella.

UNDERSTAND (uhn der STAND) *v* to know what something means

The professor asked if anyone had questions about crop rotation, and because I did not *understand*, I raised my hand.

Quiz #1

Match each word in the first column with its definition in the second column.

1.	Belief	a.	to show or think back
2.	Analysis	b.	an idea
3.	Sophisticated	c.	to think hard about something
4.	Aware	d.	a study of the basics of something
5.	Objective	e.	to guess based on hints
6.	Decision	f.	having knowledge
7.	Reflected	g.	to guess based on knowledge
8.	Understand	h.	an idea that something is true
9.	Concentrate	i.	a goal or purpose
10.	Consider	j.	to think about something
11.	Opinion	k.	an opinion; faith in something
12.	Concept	l.	to know what something means
13.	Theory	m.	a personal view or thought
14.	Estimate	n.	a final choice
15.	Inferred	o.	having high-class tastes; cultured

Quiz #2

For each question below, choose the word that is LEAST similar to the other two.

1. a. Concept   b. Theory   c. Aware
2. a. Opinion   b. Belief   c. Decision
3. a. Sophisticated   b. Analysis   c. Concentrate
4. a. Estimate   b. Reflected   c. Inferred
5. a. Consider   b. Objective   c. Understand

Puzzle #1

Using the definitions below, figure out which words you are looking for and then circle them in the Word Search. The words can be found spelled up, down, diagonally, and backwards.

```
N  J  G  B  J  E  B  T  E  O  A  C  B  E  C
O  K  O  M  C  E  T  V  A  W  A  R  E  T  O
I  W  V  D  L  W  I  A  L  N  C  C  S  A  N
N  Q  M  I  Y  T  C  Y  M  P  O  O  A  R  S
I  Y  E  B  C  O  W  S  E  I  P  M  P  T  I
P  F  B  E  N  M  I  D  Z  H  T  Z  K  N  D
O  M  J  C  B  S  S  X  I  E  L  S  L  E  E
J  B  E  D  Y  Y  C  S  C  B  Y  W  E  C  R
O  P  Q  L  H  D  T  C  X  R  I  M  Z  N  T
T  A  A  W  K  I  T  K  Z  P  A  D  J  O  H
B  N  Z  P  C  N  O  I  S  I  C  E  D  C  E
A  K  D  A  I  N  F  E  R  R  E  D  P  P  O
C  Y  T  D  N  A  T  S  R  E  D  N  U  N  R
Y  E  U  A  C  O  F  I  G  L  V  X  N  O  Y
D  X  U  Q  J  D  R  E  F  L  E  C  T  E  D
```

Definitions:

1. a study of the basics of something
2. having knowledge
3. an opinion; faith in something
4. to think hard about something
5. an idea
6. to think about something
7. a final choice
8. to guess based on knowledge
9. guessed based on hints
10. a goal or purpose
11. a personal view or thought
12. to show or think back
13. having high class tastes; cultured
14. an idea that something is true
15. to know what something means

Quiz #1 Answer Key:

1. k
2. d
3. o
4. f
5. i
6. n
7. a
8. l
9. c
10. j
11. m
12. b
13. h
14. g
15. e

Quiz #2 Answer Key:

1. c
2. c
3. a
4. b
5. b

Puzzle #1 Answer Key:

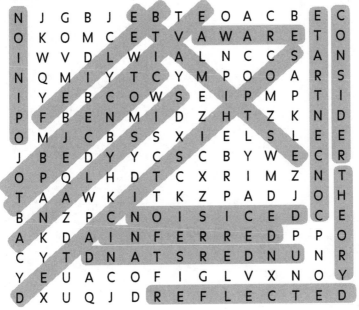

(Over, Down, Direction)
1. Analysis (1, 12, NE)
2. Aware (9, 2, E)
3. Belief (7, 1, SW)
4. Concentrate (14, 11, N)
5. Concept (7, 4, SW)
6. Consider (15, 1, S)
7. Decision (13, 11, W)
8. Estimate (13, 8, NW)
9. Inferred (5, 12, E)
10. Objective (1, 9, NE)
11. Opinion (1, 7, N)
12. Reflected (7, 15, E)
13. Sophisticated (13, 3, SW)
14. Theory (15, 9, S)
15. Understand (13, 13 ,W)

CHAPTER 4
GROWING AND SHRINKING
Words about getting bigger and smaller

ABSORB (ab SAWRB) *v* to soak in or take in

In order to *absorb* all the details of the story, Naylon leaned closer and gave his full attention.

ACCUMULATE (uh KYOO myuh leyt) *v* to gather

I noticed that after I hadn't cleaned my house for a month, the dust began to *accumulate*.

DECLINE (di KLAHYN) *v* to go downward; worsen

We witnessed the enthusiasm of the crowd quickly *decline* when they discovered that Michael Jackson was not on the premises.

DEPOSIT (di POZ it) *v* to place into something

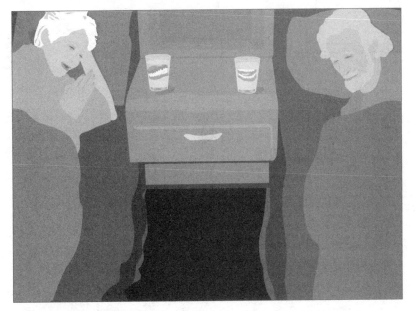

Each night, the husband and wife *deposit* their false teeth in glasses of water.

DESTROYED (di STROID) *v* torn down or ruined

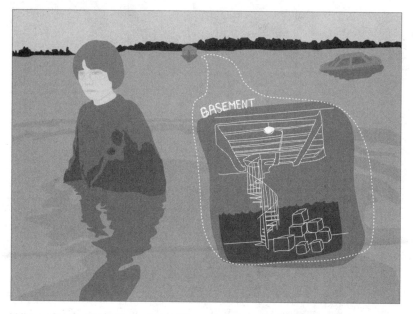

When the flood swept through town, the water leaked into our basement and *destroyed* many of our things.

DEVELOP (di VEL uhp) *v* to become more advanced

It is important for a child to share toys in order to *develop* good social skills.

ELIMINATE (i LIM uh neyt) *v* to get rid of completely

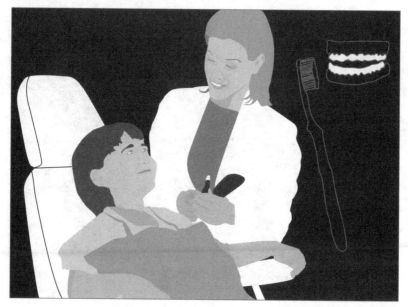

The dentist told Peter that, if he wanted to *eliminate* cavities in his mouth, he would have to brush his teeth every day.

EMERGE (i MURJ) *v* to come out

She was excited to *emerge* from the birthday cake and surprise him.

EXPAND (ik SPAND) *v* to make broader or wider

Ken ate ten slices of pizza and saw his stomach *expand*.

INCREASE (in KREES) *v* to make bigger

I found that loud noises *increase* my headaches.

LACK (lak) *n* an absence of something

I couldn't contribute to my coworker's gift due to my *lack* of money.

LIMITED (LIM i tid) *adj* within limits; restricted

The professor said that he only had a *limited* amount of time to meet with me after class.

POROUS (POWR uhs) *adj* having holes which allow liquid to go through

The *porous* roof of the old barn allowed water to drip on the cows when it rained.

PROGRESS (PROG res) *n* movement forward

Jacob could tell that he was making *progress* as a journalist when everyone complimented him on the newspaper article he had written.

STIMULATE (STIM yuh leyt) *v* to bring to action

After the markets declined, the federal reserve attempted to *stimulate* the economy by lowering interest rates.

DRILLS

Quiz #1

Match each word in the first column with its definition in the second column.

1. Deposit
2. Absorb
3. Increase
4. Destroyed
5. Stimulate
6. Eliminate
7. Accumulate
8. Expand
9. Porous
10. Emerge
11. Decline
12. Limited
13. Develop
14. Lack
15. Progress

a. to make broader or wider
b. torn down or ruined
c. to come out
d. movement forward
e. to put down into
f. within limits; restricted
g. to make bigger
h. having holes which allow liquid to go through
i. to gather
j. to get rid of completely
k. absence of something wanted
l. to soak in or take in
m. to make something more advanced
n. to go downward
o. to bring to action

Puzzle #1

Using the definitions below, figure out which words you are looking for and then circle them in the Word Search. The words can be found spelled up, down, diagonally, and backwards.

```
T  Y  N  G  B  B  D  H  X  A  K  F  M  U  V
E  E  D  H  M  M  D  E  C  L  I  N  E  F  N
T  T  N  Z  O  O  G  C  P  Z  F  H  H  E  Y
A  K  A  D  G  R  U  B  R  O  S  B  A  A  I
N  O  P  L  E  M  Z  G  O  P  S  P  E  N  F
I  D  X  M  U  O  Y  Q  G  O  O  I  C  O  F
M  E  E  L  N  M  C  O  R  D  P  R  T  F  M
I  S  A  D  V  T  I  D  E  V  E  L  O  P  N
L  T  M  R  U  W  C  T  S  A  X  C  E  U  U
E  R  L  K  B  D  I  W  S  R  K  F  N  F  S
L  O  H  C  S  M  R  E  K  T  W  X  T  Q  I
I  Y  K  A  I  I  Q  N  M  D  I  I  U  L  V
R  E  K  L  Y  S  F  K  C  B  Y  B  Y  I  Y
B  D  E  C  Q  G  G  L  D  F  A  I  A  N  O
F  X  D  A  G  Z  U  Y  F  B  W  X  C  M  P
```

Definitions:

1. to soak in or take in
2. to gather
3. to go downward
4. to put down into something
5. torn down or ruined
6. to make something more advanced
7. to get rid of completely
8. to come out
9. to make broader or wider
10. to make bigger
11. absence of something wanted
12. within limits; restricted
13. having holes which allow liquid to go through
14. movement forward
15. to bring to action

Quiz #1 Answer Key:

1. e
2. l
3. g
4. b
5. o
6. j
7. i
8. a
9. h
10. c
11. n
12. f
13. m
14. k
15. d

Puzzle #1 Answer Key:

```
T  Y  N  G  B  B  D  H  X  A  K  F  M  U  V
E  E  D  H  M  M  D  E  C  L  I  N  E  F  N
T  T  N  Z  O  O  G  C  P  Z  F  H  H  E  Y
A  K  A  D  G  R  U  B  R  O  S  B  A  A  I
N  O  P  L  E  M  Z  G  O  P  S  P  E  N  F
I  D  X  M  U  O  Y  Q  G  O  O  I  C  O  F
M  E  E  L  N  M  C  O  R  D  P  R  T  F  M
I  S  A  D  V  T  I  D  E  V  E  L  O  P  N
L  T  M  R  U  W  C  T  S  A  X  C  E  U  U
E  R  L  K  B  D  I  W  S  R  K  F  N  F  S
L  O  H  C  S  M  R  E  K  T  W  X  T  Q  I
I  Y  K  A  I  I  Q  N  M  D  I  I  U  L  V
R  E  K  L  Y  S  F  K  C  B  Y  B  Y  I  Y
B  D  E  C  Q  G  G  L  D  F  A  I  A  N  O
F  X  D  A  G  Z  U  Y  F  B  W  X  C  M  P
```

(Over, Down, Direction)

1. Absorb (13, 4, W)
2. Accumulate (10, 1, SW)
3. Decline (7, 2, E)
4. Deposit (7, 1, SE)
5. Destroyed (2, 6, S)
6. Develop (8, 8, E)
7. Eliminate (1, 10, N)
8. Emerge (3, 7, NE)
9. Expand (3, 7, N)
10. Increase (15, 4, SW)
11. Lack (4, 13, N)
12. Limited (4, 13, NE)
13. Porous (10, 5, SE)
14. Progress (9, 3, S)
15. Stimulate (9, 10, NW)

CHAPTER 5
EXTRA, EXTRA, READ ALL ABOUT IT!

Words relating to things that are extra or excessive

ABUNDANT (uh BUHN duhnt) *adj* existing in a great amount

The taxis in New York City were *abundant*, so Rebecca easily found one to take her uptown.

ADDITIONAL (uh DISH uh nl) *adj* more than what is expected

The doctor said that I should eat more vegetables, so I had an *additional* serving of green beans for dinner.

BENEFIT (BEN uh fit) *n* something good

One *benefit* of playing a musical instrument is that you can meet many people with a similar interest.

COMPLEX (kuhm PLEKS) *adj* complicated

I wanted to fix my car by myself, but I found that the inner workings were more complex than I originally thought.

EXTREME (ik STREEM) *adj* far removed from normal

Janet found that she had an *extreme* reaction to chocolate when, after taking a bite of chocolate cake, her face swelled up.

IMITATION (im i TEY shuhn) *n* a copy

At parties, I am often asked to do my *imitation* of Elvis Presley, which makes everyone laugh.

IRRELEVANT (i REL uh vuhnt) *adj* not necessary; not related

At the interview, Laszlo explained that he was a very good typist, but that was *irrelevant* to the job of a chef.

OCCASIONAL (uh KEY zhuh nl) *adj* happening on and off, or once in a while

Even though I do not like sand or water, I will take an *occasional* trip to the beach about twice a year.

REMAIN (ri MEYN) *v* to stay in place

Annoyed by our whispering during her lecture, the professor asked that we *remain* after class for punishment.

SEPARATE (SEP uh reyt) *v* to pull apart

By squeezing the nutcracker with all my might, I was able to *separate* the two halves of the walnut.

UNIQUE (yoo NEEK) *adj* singular; with no equal

My upside-down house is *unique* and unlike any other house on our block.

UNUSUAL (uhn YOO zhoo uhl) *adj* not expected; nor normal

Lily wore an *unusual* hat with feathers, flowers, and fruit sticking out of the top.

VARIOUS (VAIR ee uhs) *adj* many different things or kinds

I am well known to the *various* groups in town, such as the Book Club and the Parent–Teacher Club.

WASTE (weyst) *n* something that is not needed, extra

Max always eats every morsel on his dinner plate, because he does not want to leave any *waste*.

DRILLS

Quiz #1

Match each word in the first column with its definition in the second column.

1.	Various	a.	a copy
2.	Complex	b.	far removed from normal
3.	Occasional	c.	singular; with no equal
4.	Abundant	d.	existing in a great amount
5.	Unique	e.	to pull apart
6.	Imitation	f.	not necessary
7.	Additional	g.	something good
8.	Separate	h.	many different things or kinds
9.	Waste	i.	to stay in place
10.	Extreme	j.	something that is not needed
11.	Benefit	k.	complicated
12.	Unusual	l.	not expected; nor normal
13.	Irrelevant	m.	more than what is expected
14.	Remain	n.	happening on and off or once in a while

Quiz #2

Practice your essay writing skills by answering the following question in the space provided below. Use every word from this chapter in your response.

Question: Agree or disagree with the following statement: It is better to prepare your own food than to eat out.

Use all of these words in your response:

Abundant	Additional
Benefit	Complex
Extreme	Imitation
Irrelevant	Occasional
Remain	Separate
Unique	Unusual
Various	Waste

_____

_____

_____

_____

_____

_____

_____

_____

_____

_____

_____

_____

_____

_____

_____

_____

_____

_____

_____

_____

_____

_____

_____

Puzzle #1

Complete the crossword puzzle, below.

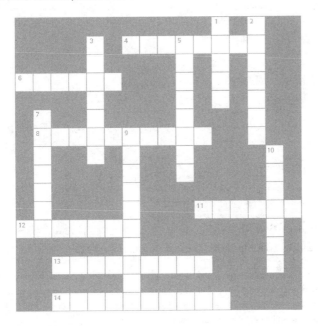

Across

4. To pull apart
6. Singular; with no equal
8. Happening on and off or once in a while
11. To stay in place
12. Far removed from normal
13. A copy
14. More than what is expected

Down

1. Something that is not needed
2. Something good
3. Not expected; nor normal
5. Existing in a great amount
7. Complicated
9. Not necessary
10. Many different things or kinds

Quiz #1 Answer Key:

1. h
2. k
3. n
4. d
5. c
6. a
7. m
8. e
9. j
10. b
11. g
12. l
13. f
14. i

Quiz #2 Answer Key:

There are many possible responses to this task. Here is a sample response.

While I do enjoy an **occasional** trip to a restaurant, I agree that it is best to prepare my own food for **various** reasons. The first **benefit** to cooking for myself is that I do not end up with any **waste**. While restaurants serve an **abundant** amount of food, I **remain** cautious about making more than I can eat in one sitting.

Some people may find my point of view **unique**, but my reasoning is not **complex**. The second benefit to preparing my own food is that I simply enjoy cooking. For example, I like to **separate** the ingredients with measuring cups and then mix them together at the end.

The third reason is that I would need an **additional** income to support a habit of eating at restaurants. While that may sound **extreme**, this point is certainly not **irrelevant** because it is important to note that eating out is very expensive.

Finally, I enjoy preparing my own food because I have **unusual** tastes, and it's difficult to find my favorite foods in restaurants. I know of one restaurant that tries to cook my favorite dish but, to me, it tastes like an **imitation**.

Puzzle #1 Answer Key:

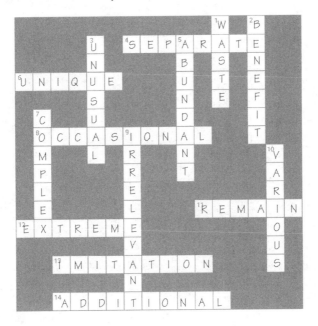

CHAPTER 6
LOOK WHO'S TALKING

Words about making statements and engaging in conversation

ANNOUNCEMENT (uh NOUNS muhnt) *n* a public statement

There was an *announcement* over the loudspeaker at the football stadium that warned people not to run onto the field.

CONCERNED (kuhn SURND) *adj* worried

When the gas tank indicated that it was empty, Juan quickly became *concerned* that his car would stop.

CONSISTS (kuhn SISTS) *v* is made up of

You can make delicious cookies with an amazingly simple recipe that *consists* of only sugar, eggs, and butter.

CONTAINS (kuhn TEYNS) *v* holds

The jar *contains* 450 jellybeans, but I guessed 229, so I lost the contest.

DEPICT (di PIKT) *v* to show in a certain way; illustrate

In his poem "The Road Not Taken," Robert Frost's timeless words *depict* the uneasiness that an individual faces when choosing between two paths.

DESCRIBE (di SKRAHYB) *v* to show with words

Each day, the apprentice would follow his master and listen to the older gentleman *describe* the process of making the items in his shop.

DISCUSS (di SKUHS) *v* to speak about with someone else

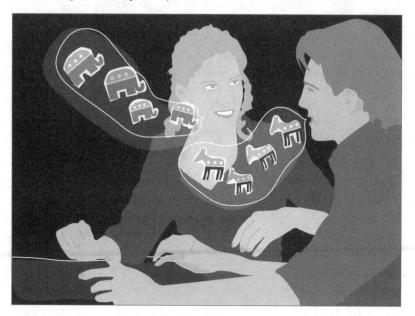

What I like about our friendship is that we can *discuss* politics calmly instead of irrationally.

INDICATE (IN di keyt) *v* to point out

When you are driving to my house, look for the stoplight, which will *indicate* where you need to turn right.

INFORMATION (in fer MEY shuhn) *n* knowledge and facts

On Erika's trip to the national park, she visited the Tourist Center to get a packet of *information* on all the popular sites.

INTRODUCE (in truh DOOS) *v* to present a person or idea to someone
for the first time

We already covered the background of Tennessee Williams, so
our literature professor will *introduce* the next topic today—
Williams's most famous plays.

MENTION (MEN shuhn) *v* to say briefly

I will try to help you fix your computer, but I should *mention* that I am certainly not an expert when it comes to programming.

PROPOSED (pruh POHZD) *v* offered up for discussion

Dan *proposed* that we eat cereal for dinner because it is his favorite food.

REFERS (ri FURS) *v* makes mention of

She *refers* to me as her closest and dearest friend, even though we just met two weeks ago.

REPRESENT (ree pri ZENT) *v* to stand in place of something else

The teacher used a cantaloupe to *represent* the size of a human brain.

SUGGEST (suhg JEST) *v* to offer an idea

I want to *suggest* that we enforce a dress code at the office because everyone shows up in jeans and T-shirts.

Quiz #1

Match each word in the first column with its definition in the second column.

1. Discuss
2. Contains
3. Represent
4. Concerned
5. Mention
6. Consists
7. Announcement
8. Information
9. Depict
10. Suggest
11. Describe
12. Indicate
13. Refers
14. Introduce
15. Proposed

a. to say briefly
b. to offer an idea
c. to stand in place of something else
d. to show with words
e. knowledge and facts
f. holds
g. to speak about with someone else
h. makes mention of
i. is made up of
j. offered up for discussion
k. worried
l. to show in a certain way
m. a public statement
n. to present a person or idea to someone for the first time
o. to point out

Puzzle #1

Using the definitions below, figure out which words you are looking for and then circle them in the Word Search. The words can be found spelled up, down, diagonally, and backwards.

```
C  O  N  T  A  I  N  S  V  I  D  A  E  C  R
Y  U  R  M  R  I  Y  B  N  E  N  V  C  O  R
I  J  Q  D  P  L  P  D  P  N  L  A  U  N  E
J  N  Q  L  C  E  I  I  O  S  E  E  D  C  P
T  W  F  Y  U  C  C  U  R  T  R  N  O  E  R
S  H  Y  O  A  T  N  B  U  S  G  B  R  R  E
E  F  J  T  R  C  W  K  W  I  R  P  T  N  S
G  Q  E  V  E  M  N  Z  R  S  E  I  N  E  E
G  H  X  M  L  X  A  K  P  N  F  Q  I  D  N
U  P  E  P  N  O  A  T  D  O  E  U  I  Y  T
S  N  S  A  V  F  Z  G  I  C  R  L  V  X  F
T  E  B  I  R  C  S  E  D  O  S  K  L  U  Z
D  I  S  C  U  S  S  H  U  F  N  O  L  W  K
Z  I  V  W  R  N  O  I  T  N  E  M  K  O  D
D  E  S  O  P  O  R  P  T  S  E  X  Z  Q  Y
```

Definitions:

1. a public statement
2. worried
3. is made up of
4. holds
5. to show in a certain way
6. to show with words
7. to speak about with someone else
8. to point out
9. knowledge and facts
10. to present a person or idea to someone for the first time
11. to say briefly
12. offered up for discussion
13. makes mention of
14. to stand in place of something else
15. to offer an idea

Quiz #1 Answer Key:

1. g
2. f
3. c
4. k
5. a
6. i
7. m
8. e
9. l
10. b
11. d
12. o
13. h
14. n
15. j

Puzzle #1 Answer Key:

```
C O N T A I N S V I D A E C R
Y U R M R I Y B N E N V C O R R
I J Q D P L P D P N L A U N E
J N Q L C E I I O S E E D C P
T W F Y U C C U R T R N O E R
S H Y O A T N B U S G B R R E
E F J T R C W K W I R P T N S
G Q E V E M N Z R S E I N E E
G H X M L X A K P N F Q I D N
U P E P N O A T D O E U I Y T
S N S A V F Z G I C R L V X F
T E B I R C S E D O S K L U Z
D I S C U S S H U F N O L W K
Z I V W R N O I T N E M K O D
D E S O P O R P T S E X Z Q Y
```

(Over, Down, Direction)
1. Announcement (12, 1, SW)
2. Concerned (14, 1, S)
3. Consists (10, 11, N)
4. Contains (1, 1, E)
5. Depict (11, 1, SW)
6. Describe (9, 12, W)
7. Discuss (1, 13, E)
8. Indicate (10, 1, SW)
9. Information (1, 3, SE)
10. Introduce (13, 9, N)
11. Mention (12, 14, W)
12. Proposed (8, 15, W)
13. Refers (11, 7, S)
14. Represents (15, 2, S)
15. Suggest (1, 11, N)

CHAPTER 7
PERSONALITY TRAITS
Words relating to character or attributes

ACCESSIBLE (ak SES uh buhl) *adj* easy to get to

The professor announced that she would make herself *accessible* by having office hours three days a week.

AVAILABLE (uh VEY luh buhl) *adj* ready; free of plans

My boss needed someone to fill in at the last minute and, luckily for him, I was *available*.

CAPABLE (KEY puh buhl) *adj* able to handle or do something

The captain assured us that, even though it was her first flight, she had been through training and was perfectly *capable* of providing a safe flight.

DIFFICULT (DIF i kuhlt) *adj* not easily done

I thought my canoeing trip would be relaxing, but I found that it was *difficult* and exhausting to paddle back upstream.

EFFICIENT (i FISH uhnt) *adj* able to get many things done with no wasted time

Simone's friends call her *efficient* because she runs errands all over town but is never late for an appointment.

EXPENSIVE (ik SPEN siv) *adj* costing a large amount of money

If you would like to visit the greatest theme park in the world, you are in for an *expensive* day of fun.

INTERESTING (IN ter uh sting) *adj* exciting, or holding one's attention

It is *interesting* to note that, although they have the same name, American and English football are very different.

INVOLVED (in VOLVD) *adj* part of something; connected

Even though I went out into the quad to study, I quickly became *involved* in a baseball game.

MOTIVATION (moh tuh VEY shuhn) *n* reason for doing something

Thomas Jefferson's *motivation* for writing much of the Declaration of Independence was to establish freedom from England.

PARTICULAR (per TIK yuh ler) *adj* singular or specific

I have a *particular* distaste for cooked fish, but I love raw sushi.

RESPONSIBLE (ri SPON suh buhl) *adj* required to do something

Because Howard accidentally left the cake out in the rain, he is *responsible* for baking a new one.

SERIOUS (SEER ee uhs) *adj* showing deep thought

The doctor determined that her stomach pains were *serious*, and that they would have to remove her appendix.

STABILITY (stuh BIL i tee) *n* steadiness in position

My lack of *stability* on skis was obvious when I came flying down the mountain with my legs over my head.·

SUCCESSFUL (suhk SES fuhl) *adj* having a good result

Sadly, the poet Emily Dickinson did not become *successful* until after her death, when much of her writing was discovered.

TECHNOLOGICAL (tek nuh LOJ i kuhl) *adj* relating to industry and science

The librarian showed us the latest *technological* advancements which would make our research process easier.

Quiz #1

Match each word in the first column with its definition in the second column.

1. Capable
2. Expensive
3. Motivation
4. Successful
5. Accessible
6. Serious
7. Available
8. Involved
9. Difficult
10. Responsible
11. Technological
12. Efficient
13. Stability
14. Particular
15. Interesting

a. not easily done
b. ready; free of plans
c. reason for doing something
d. steadiness in position
e. able to get many things done with no wasted time
f. exciting or holding your attention
g. easy to get to
h. relating to industry and science
i. singular or specific
j. able to handle or do something
k. required to do something
l. having a good result
m. part of something; connected
n. showing deep thought
o. costing a large amount of money

Quiz #2

For each question below, choose the word that is LEAST similar to the other two.

1. a. Technological   b. Responsible   c. Involved
2. a. Stability   b. Particular   c. Successful
3. a. Accessible   b. Available   c. Interesting
4. a. Motivation   b. Difficult   c. Expensive
5. a. Capable   b. Efficient   c. Serious

Puzzle #1

Using the definitions below, figure out which words you are looking for and then circle them in the Word Search. The words can be found spelled up, down, diagonally, and backwards.

```
Z  M  U  E  X  A  W  L  H  C  D  I  L  V  H
L  O  C  S  X  Y  T  I  L  I  B  A  T  S  U
V  T  V  C  E  P  M  V  V  H  C  L  U  R  U
J  I  N  T  E  R  E  S  T  I  N  G  T  A  L
D  V  L  E  L  F  I  N  G  I  T  X  C  L  N
I  A  U  E  B  W  F  O  S  Y  K  C  S  U  V
F  T  F  O  I  R  L  I  U  I  E  Z  X  C  T
F  I  S  A  S  O  I  O  C  S  V  T  S  I  Q
I  O  S  G  N  F  D  N  S  I  K  E  D  T  I
C  N  E  H  O  S  Z  I  V  R  E  Z  A  R  L
U  H  C  A  P  A  B  L  E  O  I  N  Q  A  Z
L  E  C  Y  S  L  U  I  Z  D  L  E  T  P  U
T  E  U  C  E  L  B  A  L  I  A  V  A  A  J
G  H  S  H  R  H  R  A  H  R  N  O  E  S  N
X  D  D  D  K  M  P  P  Y  O  L  S  Q  D  O
```

Definitions:

1. Easy to get to
2. Ready; free of plans
3. Able to handle or do something
4. Not easily done
5. Able to get many things done with no wasted time
6. Costing a large amount of money
7. Exciting, or holding one's attention
8. Part of something; connected
9. Reason for doing something
10. Singular or specific
11. Required to do something
12. Showing deep thought
13. Steadiness in position
14. Having a good result
15. Relating to industry and science

Quiz #1 Answer Key:

1. j
2. o
3. c
4. l
5. g
6. n
7. b
8. m
9. a
10. k
11. h
12. e
13. d
14. i
15. f

Quiz #2 Answer Key:

1. a
2. b
3. c
4. a
5. c

Puzzle #1 Answer Key:

```
Z  M  U  E  X  A  W  L  H  C  D  I  L  V  H
L  O  C  S  X  Y  T  I  L  I  B  A  T  S  U
V  T  V  C  E  P  M  V  V  H  C  L  U  R  U
J  I  N  T  E  R  E  S  T  I  N  G  T  A  L
D  V  L  E  L  F  I  N  G  I  T  X  C  L  N
I  A  U  E  B  W  F  O  S  Y  K  C  S  U  V
F  T  F  O  I  R  L  I  U  I  E  Z  X  C  T
F  I  S  A  S  O  I  O  C  S  V  T  S  I  Q
I  O  S  G  N  F  D  N  S  I  K  E  D  T  I
C  N  E  H  O  S  Z  I  V  R  E  Z  A  R  L
U  H  C  A  P  A  B  L  E  O  I  N  Q  A  Z
L  E  C  Y  S  L  U  I  Z  D  L  E  T  P  U
T  E  U  C  E  L  B  A  L  I  A  V  A  A  J
G  H  S  H  R  H  R  A  H  R  N  O  E  S  N
X  D  D  D  K  M  P  P  Y  O  L  S  Q  D  O
```

(Over, Down, Direction)
1. Accessible (14, 4, SW)
2. Available (13, 13, W)
3. Capable (3, 11, E)
4. Difficult (1, 5, S)
5. Efficient (5, 4, SE)
6. Expensive (4, 1, SE)
7. Interesting (2, 4, E)
8. Involved (7, 8, SE)
9. Motivation (2, 1, S)
10. Particular (14, 12, N)
11. Responsible (5, 14, N)
12. Serious (4, 2, SE)
13. Stability (14, 2, W)
14. Successful (3, 14, N)
15. Technological (1, 13, NE)

CHAPTER 8
THE USUAL SUSPECTS
Words having to do with the normal course of events

BASIC (BEY sik) adj simple; fundamental

One of the *basic* rules of having a dog is that you must give it exercise every day.

CERTAIN (SUR tn) *adj* free from doubt

The university administrator approved our proposal, so it is *certain* that we will have a blood drive on campus next semester.

COMMON (KOM uhn) *adj* widespread; ordinary

Eva asked the hairdresser for a different style that would not make her look so *common* and ordinary.

CONVENTIONAL (kuhn VEN shuh nl) *adj* based on general practice

Some people reject *conventional* medicine and prefer a more homeopathic approach to healing the body.

FAMILIAR (fuh MIL yer) *adj* usually known

When I was lost in the forest, it was difficult to find my way out because all the paths looked *familiar*.

FUNDAMENTAL (fuhn duh MEN tl) *adj* essential; basic

As Professor Carter explained the *fundamental* ideas behind astro-physics, I tried desperately to understand.

GENERALLY (JEN er uh lee) *adv* usually; ordinarily

Stagefright is *generally* associated with fainting or forgetting one's lines.

OBVIOUS (OB vee uhs) *adj* easily seen

I thought it was *obvious* that I was going to buy you a scarf for your birthday, so I was happy when you were genuinely surprised.

PREDICTABLE (pri DIK tuh buhl) *adj* able to be known ahead of time

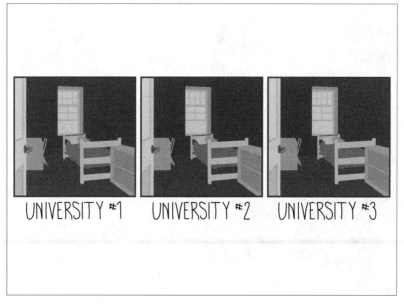

UNIVERSITY #1   UNIVERSITY #2   UNIVERSITY #3

After visiting several different college campuses, the set-up of the dorm rooms became *predictable*.

REALISTIC (ree uh LIS tik) *adj* lifelike; practical

My art teacher was impressed with my *realistic* painting of a fruit bowl.

SUITABLE (SOO tuh buhl) *adj* fitting; appropriate

I bought a huge leather chair which is *suitable* for my aching back.

TRADITIONAL (truh DISH uh nl) *adj* having to do with customs that are handed down

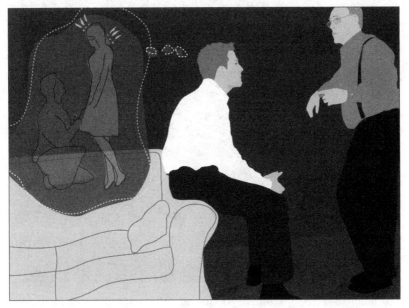

Before asking a woman to marry you, it is *traditional* in American culture to ask her father's permission.

TYPICALLY (TIP i kuhl lee) *adv* normally

I *typically* eat every meal in the dining hall, so if you can't find me, look there first.

UNIVERSAL (yoo nuh VUR suhl) *adj* applying to all

Miles loved his *universal* remote control because it turned on all of his gadgets at once.

USUALLY (YOO zhoo uhl lee) *adv* because of habit; typically

I *usually* read books very quickly, but I find myself moving through this 500 page novel unbelievably slowly.

Quiz #1

Match each word in the first column with its definition in the second column.

1. Predictable	a.	having to do with customs that are handed down
2. Traditional	b.	essential; basic
3. Common	c.	usually known
4. Generally	d.	normally
5. Basic	e.	lifelike; practical
6. Familiar	f.	simple; fundamental
7. Usually	g.	applying to all
8. Certain	h.	fitting; appropriate
9. Universal	i.	widespread; ordinary
10. Obvious	j.	able to be known ahead of time
11. Fundamental	k.	easily seen
12. Typically	l.	because of habit; typically
13. Conventional	m.	based on general practice
14. Realistic	n.	usually; ordinarily
15. Suitable	o.	free from doubt

Puzzle #1

Using the definitions below, figure out which words you are looking for and then circle them in the Word Search. The words can be found spelled up, down, diagonally, and backwards.

```
R  T  O  N  S  F  Y  F  Y  F  L  G  C  U  S
E  E  Y  S  I  L  Z  L  G  Q  A  O  K  N  U
Y  L  S  P  L  A  L  J  F  X  N  Q  H  I  O
R  C  B  A  I  A  T  A  X  V  O  Y  S  V  I
H  R  U  A  R  C  M  R  E  C  I  F  D  E  V
G  S  B  E  T  I  A  N  E  D  T  E  N  R  B
U  U  N  A  L  C  T  L  X  C  I  Y  A  S  O
Y  E  T  I  S  I  I  S  L  C  D  W  O  A  U
G  K  A  J  O  I  E  D  V  Y  A  B  K  L  A
M  R  S  N  V  B  C  B  E  I  R  D  U  Y  P
Y  V  A  C  O  M  M  O  N  R  T  L  I  I  L
X  L  I  J  K  A  J  J  E  K  P  L  Z  J  J
G  E  L  B  A  T  I  U  S  L  F  D  D  Q  R
L  A  T  N  E  M  A  D  N  U  F  B  U  S  K
R  E  A  L  I  S  T  I  C  E  V  O  E  D  D
```

Definitions:

1. simple; fundamental
2. free from doubt
3. widespread; ordinary
4. based on general practice
5. usually known
6. essential; basic
7. usually; ordinarily
8. easily seen
9. able to be known ahead of time
10. lifelike; practical
11. fitting; appropriate
12. having to do with customs that are handed down
13. normally
14. applying to all
15. because of habit; typically

Quiz #1 Answer Key:

1. j
2. a
3. i
4. n
5. f
6. c
7. l
8. o
9. g
10. k
11. b
12. d
13. m
14. e
15. h

Puzzle #1 Answer Key:

```
R T O N S F Y F Y F L G C U S
E E Y S I L Z L G Q A O K N U
Y L S P L A L J F X N Q H I O
R C B A I A T A X V O Y S V I
H R U A R C M R E C I F D E V
G S B E T I A N E D T E N R B
U U N A L C T L X C I Y A S O
Y E T I S I I S L C D W O A U
G K A J O I E D V Y A B K L A
M R S N V B C B E I R D U Y P
Y V A C O M M O N R T L I I L
X L I J K A J J E K P L Z J J
G E L B A T I U S L F D D Q R
L A T N E M A D N U F B U S K
R E A L I S T I C E V O E D D
```

```
━━━━━  ━━━━━
```

(Over, Down, Direction)

1. Basic (3, 6, SE)
2. Certain (10, 7, NW)
3. Common (4, 11, E)
4. Conventional (13, 1, SW)
5. Familiar (9, 3, SW)
6. Fundamental (11, 14, W)
7. Generally (1, 9, NE)
8. Obvious (15, 7, N)
9. Predictable (11, 12, NW)
10. Realistic (1, 15, E)
11. Suitable (9, 13, W)
12. Traditional (11, 11, N)
13. Typically (2, 1, SE)
14. Universal (14, 1, S)
15. Usually (1, 7, NE)

CHAPTER 9
CAUSE AND EFFECT
Words about leading to and arriving at results

CAUSE (kawz) *n* something that leads to a result

The *cause* of my strong odor is that I haven't showered in one week.

COMPONENT (kuhm POH nuhnt) *n* one part of something larger

An unfortunate *component* of Megan's morning routine is that she hits the "snooze" button on her alarm clock several times before getting out of bed.

DEVELOPMENT (di VEL uhp muhnt) *n* the process of growth

Because of the recent economic *development,* I was able to buy a brand new dishwashing machine.

EFFECT (i FEKT) *n* a result

One *effect* of only two hours of sleep is that you may have bags under your eyes.

FACTORS (FAK ters) *n* things that lead to a result

Two of the *factors* involved in my decision to move to the farm are that I like wearing cowboy hats and riding horses.

FORCES (fohrs) *n* things that influence or control something else

It is no secret that my parents are the *forces* behind every decision I make.

IMPACT (IM pakt) *n* the change made on one thing by another

When people make mean comments, they often do not realize the *impact* of their words on other people.

INDICATOR (IN di key ter) *n* a signal

The huge thundercloud in the sky was the first *indicator* that it would rain today.

OCCUR (uh KUR) *v* to happen

I put a piece of bread in our broken toaster oven without realizing that a fire would *occur*.

PRODUCED (pruh DOOSD) *v* made, manufactured

Honey is *produced* when bees take the nectar from flowers and bring it back to their hives.

PURPOSE (PUR puhs) *n* why something is done or used, reason

The *purpose* of telling ghost stories is to frighten everyone who is listening.

REASONS (REE zuhn) *n* causes for a belief, action, or fact

My *reasons* for getting a cat are that I want some company in my apartment, and I can't resist those big, beautiful eyes.

RESULT (ri ZUHLT) *n* something that happens because of something else, effect

Felix hadn't skated in years and, as a *result*, slipped as soon as he stepped on the ice.

ROLE (rohl) *n* a part played; a function

My boss's *role* is to critique my daily performance, assign projects to me, and hopefully give me a raise once a year.

Quiz #1

Match each word in the first column with its definition in the second column.

1. Forces   a. to happen

2. Occur   b. the process of growth

3. Factors   c. a signal

4. Cause   d. something that leads to a result

5. Reasons   e. made

6. Indicator   f. a result

7. Role   g. causes for a belief, action, or fact

8. Development   h. something that happens because of something else

9. Effect   i. things that lead to a result

10. Impact   j. a part played; a function

11. Result   k. the change made on one thing by another

12. Produced   l. one part of something larger

13. Component   m. why something is done or used

14. Purpose   n. things that influence or control something else

Quiz #2

Practice your speaking skills by answering the following question aloud. Use every word from this chapter in your response.

Question: Do you think that a student should challenge her grades if she thinks they are unfair, or should she always assume that her teachers' grading systems are fair and accurate?

Use all of these words in your response:

Cause	Indicator
Component	Occur
Development	Produced
Effect	Purpose
Factors	Reasons
Forces	Result
Impact	Role

_____
_____
_____
_____
_____
_____
_____
_____
_____
_____
_____
_____
_____
_____
_____
_____
_____
_____
_____
_____
_____
_____
_____

Puzzle #1

Complete the crossword puzzle below.

Across

4. Things that influence or control something else
5. A result
7. Causes for a belief, action, or fact
9. Made
11. One part of something larger
13. Something that leads to a result
14. Things that lead to a result

Down

1. The change made on one thing by another
2. A part played; a function
3. The process of growth
6. Why something is done or used
8. A signal
10. Something that happens because of something else
12. To happen

Quiz #1 Answer Key:

1. n
2. a
3. i
4. d
5. g
6. c
7. j
8. b
9. f
10. k
11. h
12. e
13. l
14. m

Quiz #2 Answer Key:

There are many possible responses to this task. Here is a sample response that you can read aloud to practice your speaking skills.

The **role** of every student is to question. Therefore, I think that students are justified in challenging their grades, regardless of the **factors** involved.

One **indicator** of an unfair grade is if the student studied very hard for a test and still did not do well. The **impact** of this setback could be devastating to a hardworking student. She is left wondering, "What is the **cause** of this poor grade when I studied so hard?" If she does not challenge the grade, that question will go unanswered.

Another example of an instance in which a student should challenge a grade is if he writes a paper that was poorly received. In his mind, he **produced** a masterpiece. So he is left asking, "How could this possibly **occur?**" He should ask the teacher about the **forces** behind her reasoning. He should ask if there was one **component** that lead to this grade, or if his entire paper was off the mark. His **development** as a student depends on these answers.

In conclusion, a student may have many valid **reasons** to challenge a grade and, as a **result**, the teacher should always take her seriously. Poor grades can have a devastating **effect** on a student, so it is essential that she always finds out the reasoning behind the grade. Because if a student's job is to question, and she does not fulfill that job, then she has no **purpose**.

Puzzle #1 Answer Key:

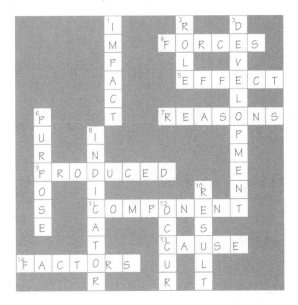

CHAPTER 10
COMPARE AND CONTRAST
Words about similarities, differences, and positions

ADJACENT (uh JEY suhnt) *adj* next to

My favorite restaurant is *adjacent* to the theatre, so I usually go to dinner there before seeing a movie.

COMBINE (kuhm BAHYN) *v* to mix together

In science class, Julie was asked to *combine* two liquids, which led to an explosion.

COMPARE (kuhm PAIR) *v* to look for or show how things are the same

You can *compare* the wings of a plane with those of a bird because both have curved topsides and flat undersides.

CONTRAST (kuhn TRAST) *v* to look for or show how things are different

In my term paper, I decided that I would *contrast* the American Congress with the British House of Parliament because the two are different in many ways.

DIFFERENCE (DIF er uhns) *n* the state of being unlike

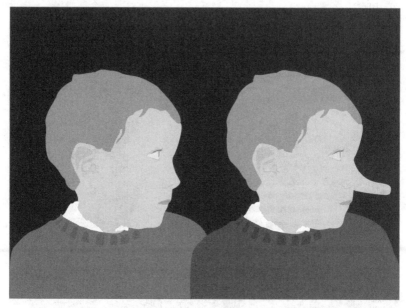

The only *difference* between my twin brother and me is that I have a very large nose.

PATTERN (PAT ern) *n* a specific order of things

We are starting to notice a *pattern* to Fred's behavior because whenever he's late for work, he has a million excuses.

POSSIBILITY (pos uh BIL i tee) *n* something that could happen

I wanted to expand my dog-walking business, so I looked into the *possibility* of creating my own website.

PREFER (pri FUR) *v* to like one over another

I *prefer* to eat chicken instead of fish because I am worried about accidentally swallowing a small bone.

PROBABLY (PROB uh blee) *adj* very likely

I told my coworker that I will *probably* ride my bicycle to the office because my car is getting repaired.

RELATED (ri LEY tid) *adj* having to do with something else

The premise of my new diet is that eating pasta sauce is directly *related* to losing unwanted pounds.

RELATIVELY (REL uh tiv lee) *adv* compared to something else

Though they are both standoffish animals, the gorilla is *relatively* more friendly than the baboon.

SIMILAR (SIM uh ler) *adj* alike

Graduate school and college are *similar* in that you have to choose a field of study, do research, and often write a final paper.

SPECIFIC (spi SIF ik) *adj* special; particular

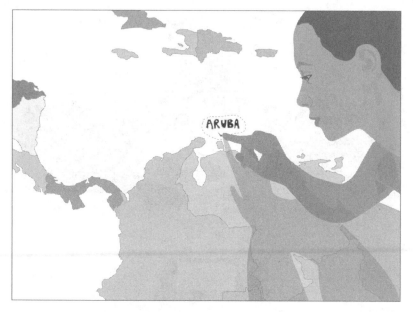

I pointed to the *specific* spot on the map where I wanted to spend my summer vacation—namely, Aruba.

SUFFICIENT (suh FISH uhnt) *adj* enough

Johann bought groceries on Monday, and assumed they would be *sufficient* for the week, but by Thursday his refrigerator was empty.

SURROUNDED (suh ROUND id) *v* closed in on all sides

When I went scuba diving, I was shocked and terrified to find myself *surrounded* by sharks.

Quiz #1

Match each word in the first column with its definition in the second column.

1. Pattern
2. Surrounded
3. Prefer
4. Similar
5. Adjacent
6. Contrast
7. Related
8. Possibility
9. Compare
10. Sufficient
11. Probably
12. Specific
13. Difference
14. Relatively
15. Combine

a. having to do with something else
b. alike
c. very likely
d. to like one over another
e. the state of being unlike
f. enough
g. next to
h. to mix together
i. special; particular
j. a specific order of things
k. something that could be true
l. to look for or show how things are different
m. compared to something else
n. to look for or show how things are the same
o. closed in on all sides

Puzzle #1

Using the definitions below, figure out which words you are looking for and then circle them in the Word Search. The words can be found spelled up, down, diagonally, and backwards.

```
M X O H S M J M L M X N Q N P
K O F S Z Y S X X S Z P W G O
J L G P O L I A U P S T M E S
E C N E R E F F I D Y C N A S
N J V C T V F X T K L I D G I
A S W I S I B O B H B J I H B
L H N F C T Z O F M A W X V I
L G R I X A U A O C B H Q M L
R M E C D L T C E X O B I J I
Z N T R D E D N U O R R U S T
T N T S A R T N O C P N O J Y
P U A K B P G A Y Y U A V U Y
P A P P S I M I L A R Q O K Z
Z I E T Q N A O F E W M M U H
A X A L G D P H C P R E F E R
```

Definitions:

1. Next to
2. To mix together
3. To look for or show how things are the same
4. To look for or show how things are different
5. The state of being unlike
6. A specific order of things
7. Something that could be true
8. To like one over another
9. Very likely
10. Having to do with something else
11. Compared to something else
12. Alike
13. Special; particular
14. Enough
15. Closed in on all sides

Quiz #1 Answer Key:

1. j
2. o
3. d
4. b
5. g
6. l
7. a
8. k
9. n
10. f
11. c
12. i
13. e
14. m
15. h

Puzzle #1 Answer Key:

```
M  X  O  H  S  M  J  M  L  M  X  N  Q  N  P
K  O  F  S  Z  Y  S  X  X  S  Z  P  W  G  O
J  L  G  P  O  L  I  A  U  P  S  T  M  E  S
E  C  N  E  R  E  F  F  I  D  Y  C  N  A  S
N  J  V  C  T  V  F  X  T  K  L  I  D  G  I
A  S  W  I  S  I  B  O  B  H  B  J  I  H  B
L  H  N  F  C  T  Z  O  F  M  A  W  X  V  I
L  G  R  I  X  A  U  A  O  C  B  H  Q  M  L
R  M  E  C  D  L  T  C  E  X  O  B  I  J  I
Z  N  T  R  D  E  D  N  U  O  R  R  U  S  T
T  N  T  S  A  R  T  N  O  C  P  N  O  J  Y
P  U  A  K  B  P  G  A  Y  Y  U  A  V  U  Y
P  A  P  P  S  I  M  I  L  A  R  Q  O  K  Z
Z  I  E  T  Q  N  A  O  F  E  W  M  M  U  H
A  X  A  L  G  D  P  H  C  P  R  E  F  E  R
```

(Over, Down, Direction)

1. Adjacent (14, 4, SW)
2. Combine (8, 9, NE)
3. Compare (9, 15, NW)
4. Contrast (10, 11, W)
5. Difference (10, 4, W)
6. Pattern (3, 13, N)
7. Possibility (15, 1, S)
8. Prefer (10, 15, E)
9. Probably (11, 11, N)
10. Related (11, 15, NW)
11. Relatively (6, 11, N)
12. Similar (5, 13, E)
13. Specific (4, 2, S)
14. Sufficient (10, 2, SW)
15. Surrounded (14, 10, W)

CHAPTER 11
LARGE AND IN CHARGE

Words relating to things that are big

CONSIDERABLE (kuhn SID er uh buhl) *adj* large; great in amount

I stared at my *considerable* amount of homework and started to cry.

DOMINANT (DOM uh nuhnt) *adj* the strongest factor or person

The Smith family likes to joke that their five-year-old daughter is the *dominant* member of the household because she always gets her way.

PROFOUND (pruh FOUND) *adj* full of knowledge; deep

I thought it was *profound* when my philosophy professor told me, "Do or do not; there is no try."

DRAMATIC (druh MAT ik) *adj* standing out; causing strong emotion

When the clown arrived at the birthday celebration, he made a *dramatic* entrance by running through the door and squeaking his rubber nose.

ESPECIALLY (i SPESH uh lee) *adv* more than is usual

Donna, who has painted every room in her house, is *especially* pleased with the color in the living room.

ESSENTIAL (uh SEN shuhl) *adj* needed the most; necessary

For Sara, an *essential* part of celebrating the holidays is for everyone in her family to gather at her grandparents' house for dinner.

IDEAL (ahy DEEL) *adj* perfect; best

The *ideal* way to disguise your appearance is to wear dark glasses, speak in a fake accent, and have a scarf cover your mouth.

IMPORTANT (im PAWR tnt) *adj* of great meaning or consequence

To conserve energy, it is *important* that you turn off all the lights when you leave the house.

MAINLY (MEYN lee) *adv* for the most part; primarily

I've *mainly* read about Sigmund Freud, so I am interested to learn about other psychiatrists and their theories.

MAJOR (MEY jer) *adj* great in size or meaning

In poker, there is one *major* rule to follow—do not let your opponents see you sweat.

NECESSARY (NES uh ser ee) *adj* needed

It is *necessary* for me to use all of my vacation days because, if unused, I lose them at the end of the year.

PRIMARY (PRAHY mer ee) *adj* happening first; main

Seamus admits to having many anxieties, but his *primary* fear is spiders.

SIGNIFICANT (sig NIF I kuhnt) *adj* worth noting; full of meaning

A *significant* number of people who suffer from migraine headaches say that the migraines cause nausea and sensitivity to light.

SUBSTANTIAL (suhb STAN shuhl) *adj* large; hard to move

I had to stay late after work because I still had a *substantial* amount of customer phone calls to make.

Quiz #1

Match each word in the first column with its definition in the second column.

1. Important	a.	of great meaning or consequence
2. Necessary	b.	great in size or meaning
3. Especially	c.	full of knowledge; deep
4. Profound	d.	needed the most; necessary
5. Substantial	e.	large; great in amount
6. Considerable	f.	happening first
7. Ideal	g.	perfect; best
8. Dominant	h.	standing out; causing strong emotion
9. Major	i.	for the most part
10. Significant	j.	needed
11. Essential	k.	worth noting; full of meaning
12. Primary	l.	the strongest factor or person
13. Mainly	m.	large; hard to move
14. Dramatic	n.	more than normally

Quiz #2

Practice your essay writing skills by answering the following question in the space provided below. Use every word from this chapter in your response.

Question: Do you agree or disagree with the following statement? You will learn all of life's most important lessons before the time you are ten years old.

Use all of these words in your response:

Considerable	Dominant
Profound	Dramatic
Especially	Essentials
Ideal	Important
Mainly	Major
Necessary	Primary
Significant	Substantial

Puzzle #1

Complete the crossword puzzle below.

Across

1. Standing out; causing strong emotion
3. Worth noting; full of meaning
10. Large; hard to move
11. The strongest factor or person
13. For the most part
14. Needed

Down

2. Large; great in amount
4. Perfect
5. Of great meaning or consequence
6. More than is usual
7. Needed the most; necessary
8. Happening first
9. Full of knowledge; deep
12. Great in size or meaning

Quiz #1 Answer Key:

1. a
2. j
3. n
4. c
5. m
6. e
7. g
8. l
9. b
10. k
11. d
12. f
13. i
14. h

Quiz #2 Answer Key:

There are many possible responses to this task. Here is a sample response.

I disagree with the statement that you learn all of life's most important lessons by the time you are ten years old. This is a **profound** thought, but it is not accurate, especially in my case. While it would have been **ideal** to learn all of my lessons early, I am well over ten years old and still have a **considerable** amount to learn.

For instance, it is **essential** for me to learn my place in society, a lesson with which I still struggle. Am I a **dominant** person, who is destined to move quickly up the ladder of success? Or am I a more reserved person, who will have slower but just as **important** road to the top? The next few years of my life will reveal these answers.

Also, I am still lacking in the **necessary** knowledge that I need in order to control my financial situation. Luckily, my **primary** income is **substantial** but, once I receive my paycheck, I don't know how to save or invest those funds. If I incorrectly manage my money, that could have a **dramatic** effect on my financial future.

Finally, while I mastered the more simple life lessons such as being selfless and caring for others, I missed out on one **major** lesson -- how to tactfully say "no" when I don't want to do something. This simple rule has had a **significant** impact on my life because I end up doing favors that people have come to expect instead of appreciate. It is **necessary** for me to learn this lesson in the next few years or else I will be living my life **mainly** for others instead of for myself.

Puzzle #1 Answer Key:

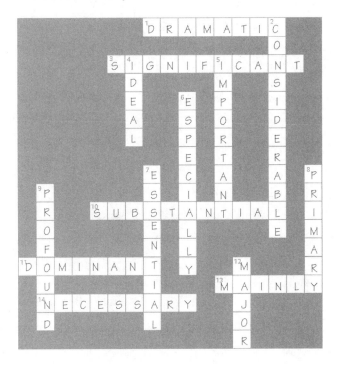

CHAPTER 12
THE NATURAL WORLD

Words about the living things around us

BEHAVIOR (bi HEYV yer) *n* someone's way of acting

Paul's *behavior* at the party showed that he was tired, so no one was surprised when he went to bed early.

CLASSIFIED (KLAS uh fahyd) *v* fit into a category

I mistakenly *classified* Jane Austen as a historian, but my professor reminded me that she was a British novelist.

CLIMATE (KLAHY mit) *n* weather

San Diego, a city that is often admired for its *climate*, remains sunny year round.

CONDITIONS (kuhn DISH uhns) *n* things that are needed; factors

I need three *conditions* to maintain my happiness: chocolate, roses, and jewelry.

CULTURAL (KUHL cher uhl) *adj* referring to the qualities of a civilization

The artist, Andy Warhol, had a *cultural* impact on society when he added his unique twist to the Pop Art genre.

ENVIRONMENT (en VAHY ruhn muhnt) *n* surroundings; settings

When I am stressed out, I go to the yoga studio, which is my favorite *environment* for relaxation.

EXIST (ig ZIST) *v* to live; to be

If he lived on Mars, he would have to *exist* on carbon dioxide.

FEATURES (FEE chers) *n* parts of someone's or something's appearance

One of the amazing *features* of the blue whale is that it is bigger than any animal on earth, including many extinct dinosaurs.

HABITAT (HAB i tat) *n* a place for living

My permanent *habitat* is on the couch, watching TV and eating potato chips.

INDIVIDUAL (in duh VIJ oo uhl) *n* something that stands alone

Because I don't like working in groups, the professor allowed me to complete the project not with others, but as an *individual*.

INHABITED (in HAB i tid) *v* lived in

Before it was discovered by explorers, Antarctica was only *inhabited* by penguins, seals, and other animal and marine life.

RITUAL (RICH oo uhl) *n* a ceremony or an act that repeats often

One American *ritual* is that most people shake hands upon meeting each other.

SITUATION (sich oo EY shuhn) *n* something's place compared to other things; circumstance

Eric found himself in an awkward *situation* when he walked into the women's restroom by mistake.

SPECIES (SPEE sheez) *n* a single class of plants or animals

While walking along the beach, we discovered a new *species* of animal with a body like a kangaroo and a head like a fish.

STRUCTURE (STRUHK cher) *n* the way something is built

The building's *structure* was weak, so it swayed with the force of the strong winds.

DRILLS

Quiz #1

Match each word in the first column with its definition in the second column.

1. Exist
2. Ritual
3. Habitat
4. Individual
5. Cultural
6. Classified
7. Structure
8. Situation
9. Behavior
10. Environment
11. Features
12. Inhabited
13. Species
14. Climate
15. Conditions

a. referring to the qualities of a civilization
b. a ceremony or an act that repeats often
c. parts of someone's appearance
d. the way something is built
e. surroundings; settings
f. a single class of plants or animals
g. something that stands alone
h. lived in
i. someone's way of acting
j. weather
k. to live; to be
l. fit into a category
m. things that are needed; factors
n. a place for living
o. something's place compared to other things

Quiz #2

For each question below, choose the word that is LEAST similar to the other two.

1. a. Climate   b. Situation   c. Environment
2. a. Behavior   b. Ritual   c. Exist
3. a. Classified   b. Inhabited   c. Habitat
4. a. Structure   b. Features   c. Cultural
5. a. Conditions   b. Individual   c. Species

Puzzle #1

Using the definitions below, figure out which words you are looking for and then circle them in the Word Search. The words are can be found up, down, diagonal, and backwards.

```
D  E  T  I  B  A  H  N  I  B  I  B  C  W  S
S  R  T  S  T  R  U  C  T  U  R  E  L  M  E
P  I  N  C  U  L  T  U  R  A  L  U  I  V  R
E  T  E  L  K  D  S  M  C  O  I  N  M  D  U
C  U  M  P  I  F  B  Y  L  D  S  C  A  N  T
I  A  N  L  A  X  C  U  A  F  Y  H  T  O  A
E  L  O  P  T  R  R  J  S  H  J  L  E  I  E
S  P  R  B  C  E  Y  M  S  A  P  P  E  T  F
O  D  I  R  V  A  R  O  I  B  F  H  A  A  I
I  N  V  R  Q  F  E  J  F  I  U  C  M  U  K
W  N  N  N  V  O  Y  C  I  T  E  A  M  T  A
K  N  E  S  F  N  H  L  E  A  I  X  I  I  R
B  E  H  A  V  I  O  R  D  T  F  O  I  S  P
I  S  N  O  I  T  I  D  N  O  C  X  O  S  N
I  N  D  I  V  I  D  U  A  L  Y  M  D  E  T
```

Definitions:

1. Someone's way of acting
2. Fit into a category
3. Weather
4. Things that are needed; factors
5. Referring to the qualities of a civilization
6. Surroundings; settings
7. To live; to be
8. Parts of someone's appearance
9. A place for living
10. Something that stands alone
11. Lived in
12. A ceremony or an act that repeats often
13. Something's place compared to other things
14. A single class of plants or animals
15. The way something is built

Quiz #1 Answer Key:

1. k
2. b
3. n
4. g
5. a
6. l
7. d
8. o
9. i
10. e
11. c
12. h
13. f
14. j
15. m

Quiz #2 Answer Key:

1. b
2. c
3. a
4. c
5. a

Puzzle #1 Answer Key:

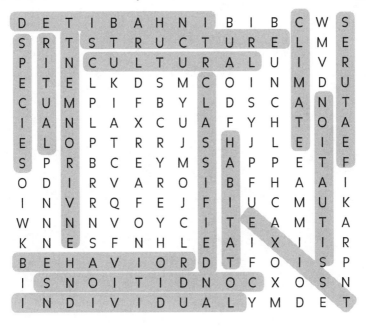

(Over, Down, Direction)
1. Behavior (1, 13, E)
2. Classified (9, 4, S)
3. Climate (13, 1, S)
4. Conditions (11, 14, W)
5. Cultural (4, 3, E)
6. Environment (3, 12, N)
7. Exist (11, 11, SE)
8. Features (15, 8, N)
9. Habitat (10, 7, S)
10. Individual (1, 15, E)
11. Inhabited (9, 1, W)
12. Ritual (2, 2, S)
13. Situation (14, 13, N)
14. Species (1, 2, S)
15. Structure (4, 2, E)

CHAPTER 13
SEEING IS BELIEVING
Words relating to your sense of sight

AESTHETICS (es THET iks) *n* visual beauty

Kristina asked her husband to shave his beard in order to preserve the *aesthetics* of their family portrait.

APPEAR (uh PEER) *v* to come into view

I granted an interview to a reporter, who told me that I would *appear* on the evening news.

CLEARLY (KLEER lee) *adv* easily seen

Elizabeth was driving home in the dark and turned on her head-lights to see *clearly*.

DISCOVERED (di SKUHV erd) *v* came upon; learned

While hiking in the woods, I turned over a rock and *discovered* a treasure box hidden underneath.

DISPLAY (di SPLEY) *v* to show

I decided to *display* my homemade jewelry outside our university's dining hall, in hopes that other students would want to purchase something.

EXPOSED (ik SPOHZD) *adj* uncovered; open to view

I don't know much about history, so I was embarrassed that my ignorance was *exposed* when the professor asked me to tell the class about Napoleon.

FOCUS (FOH kuhs) *v* to make clearer; to concentrate

Some people call me a procrastinator because, before doing my homework, I *focus* on cleaning my room from top to bottom.

IDENTIFY (ahy DEN tuh fahy) *v* to point out

The policeman asked me to *identify* the person who stole my purse, and I pointed to the woman on the left.

OBSERVE (uhb ZURV) *v* to see or watch

As part of my biology project, I had to *observe* a family of rats for five hours each day.

PERSPECTIVE (per SPEK tiv) *n* a way of seeing; point of view

When I sit in the passenger seat instead of the driver's seat, my *perspective* changes.

PORTRAYED (pawr TREYD) *v* represented with pictures, words, or actions

The actor, who *portrayed* Marilyn Monroe in the play, was embarrassed when he had to wear a dress.

PRESENCE (PREZ uhns) *n* state of being somewhere

My ex-boyfriend's *presence* at the party made me uncomfortable, so every time he came near, I headed in the other direction.

REALIZE (REE uh lahyz) *v* to understand clearly what you hadn't before

I didn't *realize* that I passed the exit on the highway until it was too late.

SURPRISED (ser PRAHYZD) *v* to come upon suddenly

I was *surprised* to learn that Abraham Lincoln, the sixteenth President of the United States, kept important papers inside his famous top hat.

VISUAL (VIZH oo uhl) *adj* having to do with sight

I found out that I am a *visual* learner, which means that I learn best when professors use the blackboard.

Quiz #1

Match each word in the first column with its definition in the second column.

1. Perspective
2. Clearly
3. Display
4. Realize
5. Visual
6. Appear
7. Identify
8. Observe
9. Aesthetics
10. Discovered
11. Portrayed
12. Presence
13. Surprised
14. Exposed
15. Focus

a. state of being somewhere
b. to come into view
c. represented with pictures, words, or actions
d. to show
e. the study of beauty
f. uncovered; open to view
g. a way of seeing; point of view
h. to point out
i. to make clearer; to concentrate
j. to come upon suddenly
k. to understand clearly what you hadn't before
l. having to do with sight
m. to see or watch
n. easily seen
o. came upon; learned

Puzzle #1

Using the definitions below, figure out which words you are looking for and then circle them in the Word Search. The words can be found spelled up, down, diagonally, and backwards.

```
S  O  Y  D  Q  K  C  A  O  M  P  E  J  B  M
F  U  X  I  M  H  V  D  I  V  V  T  M  T  V
J  D  R  S  N  I  Y  I  J  I  Q  O  W  A  W
M  N  B  P  E  L  M  S  T  V  L  F  B  J  L
S  F  C  L  R  X  A  C  V  W  I  Q  M  Y  N
U  D  J  A  E  I  E  O  A  X  Q  W  F  U  R
J  B  E  Y  P  S  V  S  G  C  I  Y  A  W
K  L  V  Y  S  L  T  E  P  U  T  B  E  X  P
C  T  R  R  A  W  H  R  D  N  C  P  A  R  K
H  Z  E  U  O  R  E  E  E  X  P  O  S  E  D
N  P  S  W  T  S  T  D  C  A  X  G  F  D  F
W  I  B  N  E  A  I  R  A  N  L  N  J  Y  Z
V  Z  O  N  B  C  C  B  O  I  K  I  C  G  H
F  Z  C  U  E  D  S  L  A  P  A  D  Z  D  D
K  E  F  O  Y  W  N  Z  C  N  M  N  L  E  W
```

Definitions:

1. the study of beauty
2. to come into view
3. easily seen
4. came upon; learned
5. to show
6. uncovered; open to view
7. to make clearer; to concentrate
8. to point out
9. to see or watch
10. a way of seeing; point of view
11. represented with pictures, words, or actions
12. state of being somewhere
13. to understand clearly what you hadn't before
14. to come upon suddenly
15. having to do with sight

Quiz #1 Answer Key:
1. g
2. n
3. d
4. k
5. l
6. b
7. h
8. m
9. e
10. o
11. c
12. a
13. j
14. f
15. i

Puzzle #1 Answer Key:

```
S O Y D Q K C A O M P E J B M
F U X I M H V D I V V T M T V
J D R S N I Y I J I Q O W A W
M N B P E L M S T V L F B J L
S F C L R X A C V W I Q M Y N
U D J A E I E O A X Q W F U R
J B E Y E P S V S G C I Y A W
K L V Y S L T E P U T B E X P
C T R R A W H R D N C P A R K
H Z E U O R E E E X P O S E D
N P S W T S T D C A X G F D F
W I B N E A I R A N L N J Y Z
V Z O N B C C B O I K I C G H
F Z C U E D S L A P A D Z D D
K E F O Y W N Z C N M N L E W
```

(Over, Down, Direction)

1. Aesthetics (7, 5, S)
2. Appear (10, 11, NE)
3. Clearly (1, 9, NE)
4. Discovered (8, 2, S)
5. Display (4, 1, S)
6. Exposed (9, 10, E)
7. Focus (13, 11, NW)
8. Identify (7, 12, NE)
9. Observe (3, 13, N)
10. Perspective (2, 11, NE)
11. Portrayed (10, 14, NW)
12. Presence (9, 8, SW)
13. Realize (8, 9, SE)
14. Surprised (1, 1, SE)
15. Visual (1, 13, NE)

CHAPTER 14
MAKE YOUR CASE
Words about making and winning arguments

ADVICE (ad VAHYS) *n* an opinion that is offered

The professor offered me *advice*, telling me what to do on the class project to get an A.

ADVISE (ad VAHYZ) *v* to offer information or an opinion

In college, the administration assigned counselors to *advise* us on important decisions.

EMPHASIZE (EM fuh syz) *v* to stress the importance of something

When speaking the English language, it is customary to *emphasize* certain syllables.

ESTABLISH (i STAB lish) *v* to put down a foundation for an idea

It is crucial for me to *establish* that I am the leader of the group, otherwise everyone else will fight for power.

EXPLAIN (ik SPLEYN) *v* to make clear; describe

Before telling you about my plans to attend culinary school, I should *explain* what led me to decide that I wanted to be a chef.

EXPRESS (ik SPRES) *v* to show your feelings with words

Some people *express* their love through words, while others show their love by giving presents.

ILLUSTRATE (IL uh streyt) *v* to make clear with examples

I would appreciate it if you could *illustrate* the differences between plant and animal cells by drawing examples of each, as I am having a hard time understanding.

IMPLY (im PLAHY) *v* to offer an idea without saying it directly; suggest

He seemed to *imply* that I am unqualified for a career in finance, even though he didn't come out and say it directly.

IMPRESS (im PRES) *v* to make someone feel good about you

When Andrew applied for a job as a magician, he tried to *impress* the interviewer with his disappearing act.

INFLUENCE (in FLOO uhns) *v* to affect the outcome

The hypnotist knew that he could *influence* my actions by saying a few words and snapping his fingers.

MAINTAIN (meyn TEYN) *v* to keep in good working order

I learned that, when I get upset, I should take deep breaths to *maintain* a sense of calm.

RESPOND (ri SPOND) *v* to answer in words

If you ask a question, please wait for me to *respond* before you interrupt with another question.

SUMMARIZE (SUHM uh rahyz) *v* to state the facts briefly

The plumber explained the problems with my sink in very technical terms, so I asked him to *summarize* his findings in more basic language.

SUPPORT (suh PAWRT) *v* to hold up from below; to aid by approving or favoring

I wanted to *support* your proposition to keep the library open year round, but I felt sorry for the people who would have to work on holidays.

Quiz #1

Match each word in the first column with its definition in the second column.

1. Emphasize
2. Express
3. Maintain
4. Support
5. Imply
6. Impress
7. Illustrate
8. Respond
9. Establish
10. Influence
11. Advice
12. Summarize
13. Advise
14. Explain

a. to put down a foundation for an idea
b. to make clear with examples
c. to stress the importance of something
d. to affect the outcome
e. to offer an idea without saying it directly
f. to state the facts briefly
g. to show your feelings with words
h. to offer information or an opinion
i. to make clear
j. to keep in good working order
k. to make someone feel good about you
l. to answer in words
m. an opinion that is offered
n. to hold up from below; to aid by approving or favoring

Quiz #2

Practice your speaking skills by answering the following question aloud. Use every word from this chapter in your response.

Question: Choose a person who you consider to be your hero and explain your choice.

Use all of these words in your response:

Advice	Advise
Emphasize	Establish
Explain	Express
Illustrate	Imply
Impress	Influence
Maintain	Respond
Summarize	Support

Puzzle #1

Complete the crossword puzzle below.

Across

2. To offer information or an option
3. To offer an idea without saying it directly
4. To make clear
8. To keep in good working order
10. To put down a foundation for an idea
11. To state the facts briefly

Down

1. An opinion that is offered
2. To affect the outcome
5. To make clear with examples
6. To make someone feel good about you
7. To hold up from below; to aid by approving or favoring
9. To show your feelings with words

Quiz #1 Answer Key:

1. c
2. g
3. j
4. n
5. e
6. k
7. b
8. l
9. a
10. d
11. m
12. f
13. h
14. i

Quiz #2 Answer Key:

There are many possible responses to this task. Here is a sample response that you can read aloud to practice your speaking skills.

My hero is my friend, Dan, for several reasons, which I will **explain**.

First, I must **establish** that he is exceedingly kind and compassionate. Most people possess some form of these traits, but it is rare to meet someone who embodies them without reservation. I cannot **emphasize** enough how caring he is.

Second, he is humble. While others attempt to constantly **impress** everyone around them, he tries to **maintain** a level-head. To **illustrate** his humility, I must mention that he received an award which he didn't tell anyone about, for fear that it would alienate others who did not receive the same recognition.

Third, he is a master of **advice**. I always turn to him when I need someone to **advise** me on many of life's important decisions. In turn, he will **express** his opinion and **imply** that I can consider his response and then form my own conclusion. He also does not **respond** with strict instructions that I must follow his advice to the letter, which I appreciate.

To **summarize**, Dan is my hero because kind, humble, and a master of advice. It is wonderful to have someone like him **support** me in life. And, fortunately, his **influence** has made me a better person.

Puzzle #1 Answer Key:

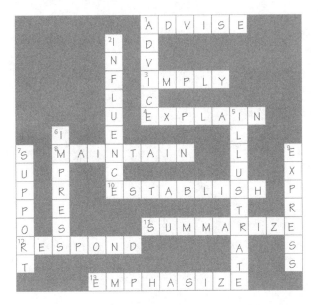

CHAPTER 15
ACTIONS SPEAK LOUDER THAN WORDS

Words relating to movement or activity

ACCEPT (ak SEPT) *v* to receive or agree to something

I decided to *accept* my brother's invitation to dinner, even though I was already full from a late lunch.

APPRECIATE (uh PREE shee yet) *v* to be thankful for; to value

Emily's children show that they *appreciate* their birthday presents by saying "thank you."

ASSISTANCE (uh SIS tuhns) *n* help

Even though I'm a terrible cook, I try to offer *assistance* in the kitchen by cleaning the pots and pans.

CONFORM (kuhn FAWRM) *v* to act the same as other people

Deidre doesn't like to stand out so, in order to *conform* with her classmates, she wears the same color socks as everyone else wears.

CONTRIBUTE (kuhn TRIB yoot) *v* to give something

I decided to run for president and, therefore, asked everyone in town to *contribute* to my campaign.

DESIGN (di ZAHYN) *v* to plan the form of something

We asked the famous architect to *design* a small house for our pet mouse.

ENGAGE (en GEYJ) *v* to get the attention of someone

In order to *engage* his audience and make them familiar with the topic, Shaker passed around a visual aid.

EXPERIENCE (ik SPEER ee uhns) *n* an event or happening

Mozart's *Clarinet Concerto* is one of my favorite pieces, so I thoroughly enjoyed the *experience* of listening to the famous clarinetist play it.

FORM (fawrm) *v* to produce or make

In art class, we learned how to *form* a piece of clay into a beautiful teapot.

INVESTED (in VEST id) *v* put money to use

Sheri *invested* in gold bars in case the economy took a downturn.

ORIGINATE (uh RIJ uh neyt) *v* to begin or start

Ranjeet had trouble deciding where to *originate* his trip around the world.

PROVIDE (pruh VAHYD) *v* to make available; give

I asked the flight attendant to *provide* me with a pillow and blanket, and she kindly agreed.

RELY (ri LAHY) *v* to depend on

I could always *rely* on my roommate to wake me up with his snoring.

REQUIRE (ri KWAHYR) *v* to need

Some people think I'm difficult because I *require* a daily foot massage.

SETTLED (SET uhld) *v* placed in order; took up residence

In 1620, the pilgrims *settled* near a large stone they called Plymouth Rock.

Quiz #1

Match each word in the first column with its definition in the second column.

1. Conform	a.	to produce or make
2. Originate	b.	to be thankful for; to value
3. Accept	c.	help
4. Form	d.	to receive or agree to something
5. Settled	e.	an event or happening
6. Provide	f.	to give something
7. Appreciate	g.	to depend on
8. Design	h.	to act the same as other people
9. Engage	i.	put money to use
10. Assistance	j.	to make available
11. Require	k.	placed in order; took up residence
12. Contribute	l.	to plan the form of something
13. Rely	m.	to begin or start
14. Experience	n.	to need
15. Invested	o.	to get the attention of someone

Quiz #2

For each question below, choose the word that is LEAST similar to the other two.

1. a. Provide   b. Settled   c. Contribute
2. a. Invested   b. Assistance   c. Experience
3. a. Rely   b. Engage   c. Require
4. a. Originate   b. Conform   c. Accept
5. a. Form   b. Design   c. Appreciate

Puzzle #1

Using the definitions below, figure out which words you are looking for and then circle them in the Word Search. The words are can be found spelled up, down, diagonally, and backwards.

```
A  B  X  F  A  M  H  Y  S  N  U  Z  T  D  B
A  P  J  O  F  P  R  L  H  E  I  T  D  T  J
K  D  R  F  A  P  P  E  N  D  O  L  W  T  Z
P  U  H  O  W  N  M  R  G  G  R  B  G  A  L
N  L  T  U  V  B  K  I  E  A  I  Z  S  P  K
A  H  V  P  D  I  T  U  C  C  G  S  C  X  J
Y  J  Z  X  E  N  D  Q  O  M  I  N  E  M  D
W  N  H  I  L  C  T  E  N  S  N  A  E  D  O
C  C  Y  S  T  X  C  R  T  K  A  E  T  Z  L
U  I  Z  D  T  W  O  A  R  S  T  Z  K  E  Z
G  B  V  E  E  C  N  E  I  R  E  P  X  E  K
R  C  L  Y  S  C  F  N  B  L  X  V  E  F  K
G  W  A  K  E  A  O  H  U  V  F  E  N  I  H
C  X  H  J  O  T  R  H  T  Y  F  X  R  I  U
Z  T  X  X  J  U  M  K  E  S  E  R  B  B  K
```

Definitions:

1. to receive or agree to something
2. to be thankful for; to value
3. help
4. to act the same as other people
5. to give something
6. to plan the form of something
7. to get the attention of someone
8. an event or happening
9. to produce or make
10. put money to use
11. to begin or start
12. to make available
13. to depend on
14. to need
15. placed in order; took up residence

Quiz #1 Answer Key:

1. h
2. m
3. d
4. a
5. k
6. j
7. b
8. l
9. o
10. c
11. n
12. f
13. g
14. e
15. i

Quiz #2 Answer Key:

1. b
2. c
3. b
4. a
5. c

Puzzle #1 Answer Key:

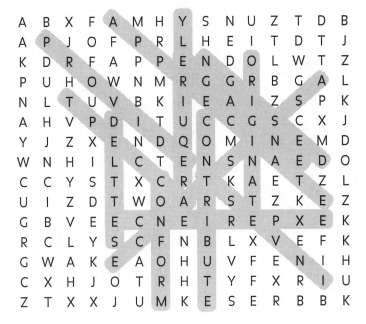

```
A   B   X   F   A   M   H   Y   S   N   U   Z   T   D   B
A   P   J   O   F   P   R   L   H   E   I   T   D   T   J
K   D   R   F   A   P   P   E   N   D   O   L   W   T   Z
P   U   H   O   W   N   M   R   G   G   R   B   G   A   L
N   L   T   U   V   B   K   I   E   A   I   Z   S   P   K
A   H   V   P   D   I   T   U   C   C   G   S   C   X   J
Y   J   Z   X   E   N   D   Q   O   M   I   N   E   M   D
W   N   H   I   L   C   T   E   N   S   N   A   E   D   O
C   C   Y   S   T   X   C   R   T   K   A   E   T   Z   L
U   I   Z   D   T   W   O   A   R   S   T   Z   K   E   Z
G   B   V   E   E   C   N   E   I   R   E   P   X   E   K
R   C   L   Y   S   C   F   N   B   L   X   V   E   F   K
G   W   A   K   E   A   O   H   U   V   F   E   N   I   H
C   X   H   J   O   T   R   H   T   Y   F   X   R   I   U
Z   T   X   X   J   U   M   K   E   S   E   R   B   B   K
```

(Over, Down, Direction)

1. Accept (8, 10, NW)
2. Appreciate (5, 1, SE)
3. Assistance (14, 4, SW)
4. Conform (7, 9, S)
5. Contribute (9, 6, S)
6. Design (14, 8, NW)
7. Engage (13, 8, NW)
8. Experience (14, 11, W)
9. Form (7, 12, S)
10. Invested (14, 14, NW)
11. Originate (11, 3, S)
12. Provide (2, 2, SE)
13. Rely (8, 4, N)
14. Require (8, 9, N)
15. Settled (5, 12, N)

CHAPTER 16
DATA AND EXPERIMENTS
Words relating to math or science

ACCURATE (AK yer it) *adj* without errors

Everyone complimented me on my performance in the game of darts, because my shots were always *accurate*.

APPROACH (uh PROHCH) *n* a way of doing something

My *approach* to cleaning the tiger's cage is to be very quiet.

ASSUMPTION (uh SUHMP shuhn) *n* a guess

My *assumption* that watering my plants every day would make them grow faster was proven incorrect when they died from too much moisture.

CRITERIA (krahy TEER ee uh) *n* factors for judgement

When searching for a babysitter, we were looking for two *criteria*—a kind personality and a driver's license.

DETERMINE (di TUR min) *v* to decide

The horse race was so close that we had to watch a playback of the video to *determine* the winner.

ELEMENTS (EL uh muhnts) *n* parts of a whole

The physics experiment required the following *elements*: weights, a pulley, and rope.

EVIDENCE (EV i dehns) *n* the thing that proves something else

The jury decided the man was guilty after seeing the most important piece of *evidence*: a broken guitar.

METHODS (METH uhds) *n* ways of doing

There are many *methods* to cooking an egg: scramble, fry, or hard boil it.

OBTAINED (uhb TEYND) *v* gathered

I *obtained* my recommendations for graduate school and included them in my admissions envelope.

PROCESS (PROS es) *n* steps for doing

The science teacher demonstrated the *process* of turning solid gold into a liquid.

PROJECT (PROJ ekt) *n* a task; plan

To prepare a presentation about customer service, I was forced to work on a joint *project* with a coworker that I didn't like.

RANGE (reynj) *n* the extent or amount of something

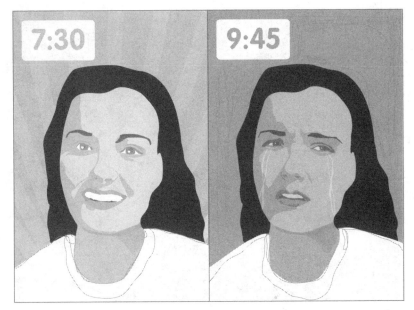

On any given day, Cassandra's emotions *range* from incredibly happy to very sad.

RESEARCH (ree SURCH) *v* to search for information

I spent all day in the library doing *research* on William Shakespeare for my English class.

TECHNIQUE (tek NEEK) *n* method of performance, procedure by which a task is accomplished

My tennis game finally improved when I mastered the *technique* of serving.

VALUE (VAL yoo) *n* the importance or worth assigned to something

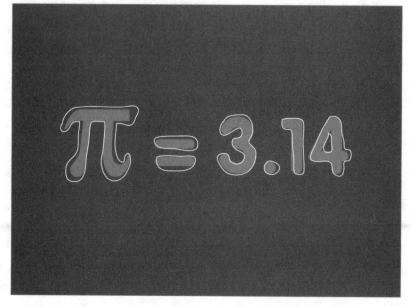

One number that I can never forget is the *value* of pi, 3.14.

Quiz #1

Match each word in the first column with its definition in the second column.

1. Project   a. a way of doing; method of performance
2. Value   b. factors for judgment
3. Methods   c. to search for information
4. Approach   d. the importance or worth assigned to something
5. Research   e. the extent of something
6. Accurate   f. gathered
7. Process   g. to decide
8. Criteria   h. a way of doing something
9. Evidence   i. does not have errors
10. Technique   j. parts of a whole
11. Range   k. a task; plan
12. Assumption   l. a guess
13. Elements   m. ways of doing
14. Determine   n. the thing that proves something else
15. Obtained   o. steps for doing

Puzzle #1

Using the definitions below, figure out which words you are looking for and then circle them in the Word Search. The words can be found spelled up, down, diagonally, and backwards.

```
P  Q  J  O  N  V  Q  E  T  I  H  W  C  D  M
R  L  M  F  O  H  A  N  G  O  M  R  Y  E  K
O  P  Q  E  I  Y  K  C  Z  N  I  L  E  N  A
C  U  J  O  T  P  D  E  C  T  A  Z  U  I  P
E  Y  G  J  P  H  X  T  E  U  E  R  L  A  P
S  H  F  Y  M  G  O  R  I  N  R  U  A  T  R
S  C  K  E  U  N  I  D  I  L  E  A  V  B  O
E  V  V  X  S  A  S  M  S  R  E  N  T  O  A
Z  C  R  E  S  W  R  M  Y  A  L  O  N  E  C
I  W  N  M  A  E  S  T  N  E  M  E  L  E  H
G  X  X  E  T  E  C  H  N  I  Q  U  E  E  F
F  T  Y  E  D  F  L  U  T  J  Q  M  G  K  H
M  O  D  S  U  I  T  C  E  J  O  R  P  Z  D
X  T  M  Q  R  U  V  N  L  T  J  X  F  A  C
C  O  I  F  W  I  R  E  S  E  A  R  C  H  B
```

Definitions:
1. Does not have errors
2. A method of performance
3. A guess
4. Factors for judgment
5. To decide
6. Parts of a whole
7. The thing that proves something else
8. Ways of doing
9. Gathered
10. Steps for doing
11. A task; plan
12. The extent of something
13. To search for information
14. A way of doing; method of performance
15. The importance or worth assigned to something

Quiz #1 Answer Key:

1. k
2. d
3. m
4. h
5. c
6. i
7. o
8. b
9. n
10. a
11. e
12. l
13. j
14. g
15. f

Puzzle #1 Answer Key:

```
P  Q  J  O  N  V  Q  E  T  I  H  W  C  D  M
R  L  M  F  O  H  A  N  G  O  M  R  Y  E  K
O  P  Q  E  I  Y  K  C  Z  N  I  L  E  N  A
C  U  J  O  T  P  D  E  C  T  A  Z  U  I  P
E  Y  G  J  P  H  X  T  E  U  E  R  L  A  P
S  H  F  Y  M  G  O  R  I  N  R  U  A  T  R
S  C  K  E  U  N  I  D  I  L  E  A  V  B  O
E  V  V  X  S  A  S  M  S  R  E  N  T  O  A
Z  C  R  E  S  W  R  M  Y  A  L  O  N  E  C
I  W  N  M  A  E  S  T  N  E  M  E  L  E  H
G  X  X  E  T  E  C  H  N  I  Q  U  E  E  F
F  T  Y  E  D  F  L  U  T  J  Q  M  G  K  H
M  O  D  S  U  I  T  C  E  J  O  R  P  Z  D
X  T  M  Q  R  U  V  N  L  T  J  X  F  A  C
C  O  I  F  W  I  R  E  S  E  A  R  C  H  B
```

(Over, Down, Direction)

1. Accurate (7, 2, SE)
2. Approach (15, 3, S)
3. Assumption (5, 10, N)
4. Criteria (13, 1, SW)
5. Determine (3, 13, NE)
6. Elements (14, 10, W)
7. Evidence (8, 15, NW)
8. Methods (3, 2, SE)
9. Obtained (14, 8, N)
10. Process (1, 1, S)
11. Project (13, 13, W)
12. Range (12, 5, NW)
13. Research (7, 15, E)
14. Technique (5, 11, E)
15. Value (13 ,7, N)

CHAPTER 17
IT'S ABOUT TIME
Words about the past, present, and future

APPROXIMATELY (uh PROK suh mit lee) *adv* close to; about

Jane has *approximately* thirty minutes to eat lunch when she's rushing between classes.

CEASED (seesd) *v* stopped

When we gave the children ice cream, they immediately *ceased* crying.

CONTEMPORARY (kuhn TEM puh rer ee) *adj* modern; happening at the same time

Because we're a *contemporary* couple, I proposed to my husband instead of the other way around.

CONTINUE (kuhn TIN yoo) *v* to go on after stopping

After putting out a small fire in the kitchen, I decided to *continue* eating dinner.

CURRENT (KUR uhnt) *adj* happening now

I read the newspaper every day so that I can stay informed about *current* events.

EVENTUALLY (I VEN choo uh lee) *adv* at some time in the future

After seven long days in the desert, the explorer was relieved when he *eventually* found water.

FREQUENTLY (FREE kwuhnt lee) *adv* often

Gene *frequently* eats peanut butter and marshmallow sandwiches because they are his favorite.

GRADUAL (GRAJ oo uhl) *adj* slow

My climb up the mountain was at a *gradual* pace because I was carrying a fifty-pound backpack.

IMMEDIATELY (i MEE dee it lee) *adv* now; at once; right away

When my friend told me I had spaghetti sauce all over my face, I *immediately* reached for a napkin.

INEVITABLE (in EV I tuh buhl) *adj* sure to happen

It is *inevitable* that when I study hard for a test, I will receive a better grade than if I hadn't studied at all.

RAPID (RAP id) *adj* happening quickly

Because I hadn't been washing my face every day, the dermatologist noticed a *rapid* decline in the health of my skin.

RARELY (RAIR lee) *adv* not often; seldom

Shirley *rarely* performs this song, so when we asked her to sing, she forgot the lyrics.

RECENTLY (REE suhnt lee) *adv* not long ago

Because it had snowed *recently*, the sidewalks were slippery.

SCHEDULE (SKEJ ool) *n* a list of activities or plans

Kay wanted to pull her hair out in frustration because her busy *schedule* did not allow time for relaxation.

TERM (turm) *n* a part of the school year or a limited period of time; also, a word used for a particular thing

At the end of the *term* I graduated, which is another *term* for finishing school.

Quiz #1

Match each word in the first column with its definition in the second column.

1. Contemporary
2. Inevitable
3. Recently
4. Eventually
5. Gradual
6. Approximately
7. Term
8. Current
9. Schedule
10. Ceased
11. Rarely
12. Frequently
13. Immediately
14. Continue
15. Rapid

a. sure to happen
b. a list of activities or plans
c. close to
d. often
e. happening now
f. modern; happening at the same time
g. happening quickly
h. stopped
i. not often; seldom
j. slow
k. to go on after stopping
l. a part of the school year; also another word for something else
m. now; at once
n. not long ago
o. at some time in the future

Quiz #2

Practice your essay writing skills by answering the following question in the space provided below. Use every word from this chapter in your response.

Question: Agree or disagree with the following statement: If someone is given one million dollars, he or she should save the money instead of spending it.

Use all of these words in your response:

Approximately	Ceased
Contemporary	Continue
Current	Eventually
Frequently	Gradual
Immediately	Inevitable
Rapid	Rarely
Recently	Schedule
Term	

Puzzle #1

Complete the crossword puzzle below.

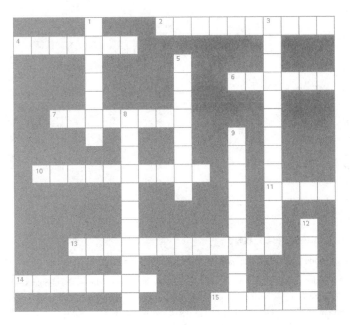

Across

2. At some time in the future
4. Slow
6. Not often; seldom
7. To go on after stopping
10. Often
11. A part of the school year; also another word for something else
13. Modern; happening at the same time
14. A list of activities or plans
15. Stopped

Down

1. Happening now
3. Close to
5. Not long ago
8. Now; at once
9. Sure to happen
12. Happening quickly

Quiz #1 Answer Key:

1. f
2. a
3. n
4. o
5. j
6. c
7. l
8. e
9. b
10. h
11. i
12. d
13. m
14. k
15. g

Quiz #2 Answer Key:

There are many possible responses to this task. Here is a sample response.

I disagree with the idea that if someone is given one million dollars he or she should save the money. That should only be the last step. In fact, if I were given one million dollars, I would first travel and shop. Only after spending half of my money would I start saving.

First, I would like to travel, which would be convenient because my **current** school **term** is coming to a close. I have **recently** become aware that there are several places around the world that I would like to visit, such as Costa Rica, Hawaii, Ireland, and Germany. If I were given the money to travel, I would start in Costa Rica and **continue** along to the other destinations at a **gradual** pace. It is **inevitable** that after visiting these wonderful locales, I may never want to return home!

The second thing I would do with my money is shop. I can already picture myself in a **rapid** race around the shopping mall, grabbing everything in sight. I **rarely** have enough money to splurge on expensive clothes, so I would **immediately** head to my favorite stores. In my happy state, I would purchase the most **contemporary** outfits and **frequently** return to the mall to update my wardrobe.

Finally, when I **ceased** my frantic **schedule** of nonstop spending, I would start saving. I would put **approximately** half of my one million away in the bank and then continue splurging with whatever was left over. If I did not make this decision, I would **eventually** be left penniless.

Puzzle #1 Answer Key:

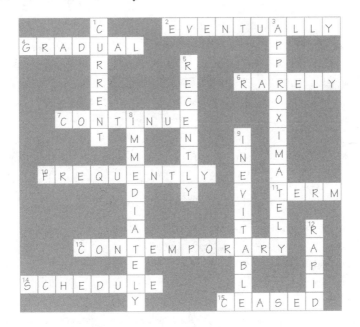

Index

A
absorb
abundant
accept
accessible
accumulate
accurate
adapt
additional
adjacent
advantage
advice
advise
aesthetics
affect
alternative
analysis
announcement
appeal
appear
appreciate
approach
approximately
argue
assistance
assumption
available
aware

B
basic
behavior
belief
benefit

C

capable
cause
ceased
certain
classified
clearly
climate
combine
common
compare
complex
component
concentrate
concept
concerned
conditions
conflict
conform
consider
considerable
consists
contains
contemporary
continue
contradict
contrast
contribute
conventional
convince
criteria
critical
cultural
current

D

decision
decline
depict
deposit
describe
design
destroyed
determine
develop

development
difference
difficult
discovered
discuss
display
diversity
dominant
dramatic

E

effect
efficient
elements
eliminate
emerge
emphasize
encourage
engage
ensure
environment
especially
essential
establish
estimate
eventually
evidence
evolve
except
exist
expand
expensive
experience
experiment
explain
exposed
express
extreme

F

factors
familiar
features
fluctuate
focus
forces
form
frequently
fundamental

G

generally
gradual
habitat

I

ideal
identify
illustrate
imitation
immediately
impact
imply
important
impress
improve
increase
indicate
indicator
individual
inevitable
inferred
influence
information
inhabited
innovations
interesting
introduce
invested
involved
irrelevant

L

lack
limited

M

mainly
maintain
major
mention
methods
migrate
motivation

N

necessary

O

objective
observe
obtained
obvious
occasional
occur
opinion
oppose
originate

P

particular
pattern
perspective
porous
portrayed
possibility
predictable
prefer
presence
prevent
primary
probably
process
produced
profound

progress
project
promote
proposed
prove
provide
purpose

R
range
rapid
rarely
realistic
realize
reasons
recently
reduced
refers
reflected
related
relatively
rely
remain
replaced
represent
require
research
resist
respond
responsible
result
ritual
role

S
schedule
separate
serious
settled
significant
similar
situation
sophisticated
species

specific
stability
stimulate
structure
substantial
successful
sufficient
suggest
suitable
summarize
support
surprised
surrounded

T
technique
technological
term
theory
traditional
transformed
typically

U
understand
unique
universal
unusual
usually

V
value
various
vary
visual

W
waste

About the Author

Vanessa Coggshall holds a Bachelor's degree from Rutgers University and a Master's degree from The College of New Jersey, both in English Literature. For over nine years, Vanessa has worked as a course director, product developer, project editor, teacher, and tutor with The Princeton Review, where her name is synonymous with the TOEFL. At the same time, Vanessa is an Adjunct Professor of English Composition at various colleges in New Jersey and Pennsylvania, helping many ESL students improve their writing. In her free time, Vanessa likes to read captivating books, spend time with her dog, Piper, and eat good sushi (not all at the same time).

Notes

Notes

Notes